Advance Praise for *Speak Like Yourself... N*

No matter what your position, no matter what your job, we all have to communicate—and this book will take you to the next level of success.

—**Anne Loehr**, Author, Executive Coach, and Keynote Speaker (named "Generational Guru" by *The Washington Post*)

A must-read for any business professional. Jezra is a speaker coaching guru, and this book will boost your public speaking skills, whether you're a beginner or an expert.

—**Jeremy Masters**, Founder & Managing Partner, *Worklogix*

Jezra's advice and wisdom make public speaking easy and authentic. She'll help you create an experience that not only meets your goals but is enjoyable, too!

—**Adelaide Lancaster**, Business Coach, and Co-Founder, *In Good Company Workplaces*; Co-Author, *The Big Enough Company*

If you want to get started as a speaker or improve your presentation skills, this book is for you. Jezra's explanations, tips and examples are clear and easy to understand. She has a natural warmth and down-to-earth style that'll make you feel like she's your own private coach.

—**Dana Rubin**, Director, *New York Speechwriter's Roundtable*

Is there anything new under the sun for public speakers since Demosthenes addressed the roaring sea with pebbles in his mouth? Maybe not; but if you're looking for a clear understanding of the subject, presented in an engaging manner, look no further.

—**Charles di Cagno**, Director, *Public Speaking Center of NY*

I've presented more than 30 keynote speeches this year, and the feedback and advice I received from Jezra was invaluable. Now, with the publication of her book, so many will have the opportunity to benefit by simply reading and putting her easy-to-employ advice to use.

—**Ted Rubin**, Chief Social Media Officer, *Collective Bias* (80,000+ Twitter followers)

Speak Like Yourself... No, Really!

Follow Your Strengths and Skills to Great Public Speaking

Jezra Kaye

NEW YORK

Library of Congress Control Number 2012943822

ISBN 978-0-9793527-2-0

Design by Jonathan Fulton

3Ring Press books are available at special discounts
when purchased in bulk for premium and sales
promotions as well as for fund-raising or educational
use. For details, contact info@3ringpress.com

3Ring Press
191 St. Marks Avenue
Brooklyn, NY 11238

3RingPress.com

Printed in the United States of America
First printing September 2012

10 9 8 7 6 5 4 3 2 1

This book is dedicated to my clients:
You inspire me every day!
And "same as it ever was," to my husband **Jerome Harris**
and our daughter **Laurika Harris-Kaye**, with love.

My deepest thanks and appreciation go to:

My talented production team, Jon Fulton (book designer) and
Carol Goldberg (illustrator): You are every author's dream.

The incredible women of my Writer's Group—Rose Rubin Rivera, Anne Lopatto,
and Mary Moreno—who critiqued draft after draft after draft of this book:
Here's to *your* books, and our next 15 years together!

My web strategist "Rebbe" Melea Seward (Founder, *Chief Amusement Designer
and Board of Us*), who always manages to coax me to the next level of success.

My MBTI trainer, Hile Rutledge (CEO, *Otto Kroeger Associates*), for his feedback
on Appendix C. Any errors or flights of interpretive fancy are mine alone.

Colleagues Ilise Benun (Co-Founder, *Marketing Mentor*); Sam Horn (Intrigue
Agent and author of *POP!*); and Diane O'Connell (Editorial Director, *Write to
Sell Your Book*), for generously contributing to this book's title; and Adelaide
Lancaster and Amy Abrams (Co-Founders, *In Good Company Workplaces*), for
your encouragement and example.

My Sales Associate Lori Kettles, for helping get the word out.

The SET™ Corporation, for the images that illustrate Chapter 6,
and permission to use them.

Table of Contents

› Introduction

Don't Jump!

› The Public Speaking Emergency

Before I became a public speaking coach, I had no idea there was such a thing as a public speaking emergency.

Sure, I knew that people get asked, at the last minute, to offer a toast.

But I didn't expect that I would be getting calls from people who *suddenly realized* that they were going to be addressing an audience of 1000 in three days, or speaking in Brussels next Tuesday and could we please make an appointment *now!*

› Take the Stairs

People go into denial about their public speaking commitments because they literally don't know what else to do. They don't have a plan for how to prepare, or a method that will ensure success.

Imagine that you're standing at the edge of a cliff, with a rocky canyon far below and another cliff face opposite. Your job (sometimes called "making a speech") is to get to the opposite cliff, hopefully with your audience in tow.
It seems to many people that the only way to get there is to jump—and maybe fall and die.

But wait. Don't jump. Look down at your feet.

There's a path carved into the cliff-face, complete with stairs, that you can use to complete this journey—and **this book is that path!**

By following its step-by-step instructions, you'll be able to prepare, practice, and present a speech that delights your audience, makes you proud, and fulfills your business and personal goals.

› How to Use This Book

Speak Like Yourself... No, Really! was written to be read straight through, with each chapter building on the last.

But many chapters also stand alone. So if something particularly interests you, feel free to open the book there, and go back to fill in the blanks as needed.

Whatever your order of reading, though, be sure to play with these ideas. Public speaking is an active skill, and it's through action—through trying, experimenting, embracing, exploring, and yes, speaking in public—that *your* skills will grow.

Have fun, and let me know how it goes!

Jezra Kaye
Brooklyn NY
jezra@speakupforsuccess.com

Chapter 1

To Be Or Not To Be... *Me!*

I've coached hundreds of people on their communications skills.

They've come from diverse professions and perspectives, from different cultures and countries. Some have worked on high-stakes speeches; others, on how to sound more polished; still others, on how to overcome their fears.

But most of them have had one thing in common: They thought the way they spoke was **wrong**.

Before we jump into the tips, tricks, and techniques that will help you become a happy, confident, and successful public speaker, let's get that one out of the way!

"I *Should* Speak Differently."

When I hear that from one of my public speaking clients, I usually ask, "Yeah? What are you doing that you don't like?"

"Well," they say, "I **should**..."

Use bigger words	Sound more passionate
Use longer sentences	Sound less emotional
Not hesitate so much	Make more eye contact
Not move around so much	Look more serious
Move around more	Be more relaxed
Not use my hands	Be funny
Use my hands more	Not feel scared
Not speak from notes	Not feel awkward
Use PowerPoint	Not have any feelings of self-doubt
Not use PowerPoint	Not make any mistakes

(And the list goes on. And on.)

> Who Made Those Rules?!!

No wonder so many people hate the thought of public speaking! How can you not hate something that requires you to (a) perform perfectly, (b) follow a long list of nit-picky rules, and (c) never have an unpleasant or uncomfortable feeling while you're doing it?

I must have slept through the English class where they passed out the memo with all those rules. So, luckily for me, I always figured that, if I was talking and the other person was still awake and seemed to be following what I said, I must be saying it just fine.

This doesn't mean there are no rules. It just means that you're free to follow the rules that work for you, and ditch the ones that don't.

Here are *my* rules for public speaking:

Jezra's Public Speaking Rules

- Don't lie to your audience, even when it's really tempting.
- Stay focused on what matters to them. (In Chapter 3, you'll learn how to figure out what matters to your audience.)
- Do your best to put your own ego and insecurities aside (trust me, you'll be able to pick them back up later!) and connect with the people you're talking to. (This is addressed in Chapters 10 and 11.)

Notice that there's nothing in these rules about grammar, diction, sentence structure, or any of the myriad shoulds that bedevil my clients. They're about how to conduct a relationship with your audience. That relationship, and how to build it, is the subject of much of this book.

Why You Should Never Lie to Your Audience
(WARNING: Animals were hurt in the making of this story)

In the 1990s, I coached a research scientist at a big pharmaceutical company for a speech he was going to give. He was a reasonably nice guy, but his job was to report on tests that measured the reaction of dogs to a new prescription drug (which translates into: how much do you have to give them before they get *really, really* sick?).

Clearly, this was a sensitive topic, and my client was desperate to charm his audience. So he asked me, "How about if I tell people that the dogs got adopted and are living happily ever after?"

I shook my head sadly. "You can't say that, because the dogs are dead."

"What do you mean?" he asked, trying to fake through the moment.

"Weren't the dogs autopsied?"

"Well, yeah, but..."

"But nothing, " I told him. "You can't say the dogs are happy if the dogs are dead."

He ended up saying nothing about the dogs (good choice), and saved himself from looking like either a liar or a fool.

You can save yourself from missteps, too, by deciding that you'll never lie to an audience—even when it's really tempting.

> Your Strengths as a Communicator

Whether you follow my "rules" or your own, I hope you're beginning to agree that trying to meet an impossible, externally-imposed standard of perfection is **not** the best way to become a great public speaker!

In this book, we're going to take a different path to that goal—one that moves you toward being more powerfully and relaxedly *yourself* when you communicate with others.

You're the key to this whole process. So, before you read any further, let's find out a little more about *you*. Please write your answer to the following question on the numbered lines below.

Question: *What are three of the strengths, skills, or traits that make (or will make) you a good communicator?*

The samples that follow are to prompt your thinking.

Sample Communications Strengths and Skills

Are you:	**Do you have a:**
Logical?	Great smile?
Sincere?	Relaxed manner?
Funny?	Commanding voice?
Well-organized?	Interesting viewpoint?
Good with detail?	Good education?
Willing to take a risk?	Quick wit?

A Few of My Communications Strengths or Skills

1 _____

2 _____

3 _____

Now, tell the truth: How long did that take?

Ten seconds? Ten minutes? *Hell will freeze over before you think of anything good to say about your own communication skills?*

I've found that, if I ask 100 people to do this exercise, only a few can do it without waging a sometimes heroic internal struggle. Many people can't do it, period.

Yet, if I asked these same people to list three skills or strengths that make them good neighbors, or good workers, or good parents, or good friends, I'm guessing they would be able to list *something*.

Isn't it sad that, after a lifetime of communicating with other people, many of us can't think of *even one good thing* to say when we're asked to describe our communications strengths?

Responsibility for that sad situation probably goes to...

> That Self-Critical Little Voice in Your Head

Have you ever been heckled while you were presenting? It's not a pleasant experience—and it's even less pleasant when the heckling comes from a nasty, sneering, self-critical voice that's living in what should be a safe space: your mind.

You probably know the voice I'm talking about, right?

As far as I can tell, most people have that little voice to either a large or small degree. It warbles in your ear, telling you in no uncertain terms that you're falling short and headed for a major crash-and-burn.

This is the voice that drives people to drink, to despair, or to violence. Its only real function is to suck the life force out of you and leave an empty shell behind. (Yes, I've seen *Invasion of the Body Snatchers!*)

> ### Is it OK to Speak Up for Success?
>
> Nine times out of 10, the conversations I have with my clients aren't really about whatever public speaking rules they think they're breaking. Nine times out of 10, what they really want to know (whether they ask the question this way or not) is: *Is it OK for me to speak up? Do I have the "right" to be heard, loud and clear?*

You can think of this nasty little parasitic voice as your "superego" (Sigmund Freud), your "critical parent" (Eric Berne), or the sound of "cruel self-rebuke" (advice columnist Cary Tennis).

But however you think of your own personal Nasty Little Voice (NLV), I beg you, **do not** think of it as your speaker coach.

It **doesn't have a clue** about how to give great presentations!

> Who You Gonna Call? Your Avatar!

Almost everyone has a personal NLV.

Many people spend their lives trying to limit the damage this "critic" can inflict. Other people spend their lives trying to deflect the NLV by defending themselves or attacking others.

All of which takes time and energy that you, as a public speaker, can't afford.

> **Useful Critique vs. Nasty Little Voice**
>
> Useful feedback, whether it comes from your own mind or from the outside world, is matter-of-fact and non-blaming. But the stuff from your NLV makes you want to squirm, hide (preferably by disappearing through the floor), or become somebody else.
>
> That's how you tell the difference between feedback that that has actual constructive value, and a "feedback" from your NLV: If you're thinking something that makes you want to squirm, hide, or become somebody else, this is, *by definition*, a NLV stealth attack.

How do you handle the NLV? It's hard to kill, it's hard to keep quiet, and it's particularly hard to ignore. So I suggest you end-run the whole issue by creating your own personal public speaking **Avatar**.

Now by Avatar, I don't mean a Hindu god; nor do I mean the animated movie with that name. For those of you who grew up before the advent of video games, an Avatar is the personality, or *persona*, that a gamer takes online. Think of it as a character in a play or movie that's all about you.

In fact, this Avatar really *is* you—but it's "you" as you want to be seen by others. "You" in a powerful, more concentrated form. "You" with the messy parts weeded out.

An Avatar is your quintessential "best self." It is, to use a marketing phrase, *the truth about you, told well.*

› How I Learned to Stop Worrying and Trust My Avatar

When I go out to do a speech, or pitch, or interview, there are two people I can send to get the job done. Both of them are smart, warm, hard-working, and sincere. They're experts in the same areas, and share identical points of view; but they do differ in important ways.

Let's call one of them **Jezra**.

Jezra is complicated, vulnerable, often anxious, and prone to hiding in bed with a romance novel and a double scotch. She can be impatient, imperious, and judgmental. She's been known to pick stupid fights with her husband, and feels incredibly, irrationally insecure whenever she's faced with a new work challenge. She can sometimes be focused, poised, calm, confident, and amazingly patient.

Jezra's Avatar counterpart is called ⋆**JEZRA**⋆.

⋆**JEZRA**⋆ is focused, poised, calm, confident, and amazingly patient. Period.

Since I am actually both of these people, the choice of who to send to a meeting or presentation is up to me. Usually, I send ⋆**JEZRA**⋆ when I want to present a calm, confident, and consistent face to the world.

Is This Avatar Thing Hypocrisy?

I don't think so. I think of it as good editing, since I'm editing out parts of myself that don't bring anything positive to the situation I'm in.

If you worry that invoking an Avatar is dishonest, you can let that worry go. Unless you're a sociopath, your full and true personality will gradually slip out around the edges of the Avatar you create, and make you a charming and intriguing enigma.

Your Avatar doesn't hide the real you. It just gives you a more powerful and confident place to stand while you're learning new things, or performing stressful tasks.

› You Already Have an Avatar

Without knowing it, you've already begun to think about the qualities you might assign to your Avatar.

Remember the three communications strengths or skills that you wrote down? These existing strengths and skills—real qualities that you already take pride in—can become the basis for your Avatar, and the public speaker you want to be.

Since you're going to spend a lot of time with your communications Avatar, you should create one that you can really commit to. So here's the question: Do the items on your list reflect things that you genuinely like and admire about yourself and other public speakers you've heard? Or are they qualities that you think *should be* on the list?

If you haven't come up with anything yet, imagine what your best friend would say. Or **make this an aspirational exercise** and write down the three or four strengths or skills that you would **like to be known for**, when you've reached your public speaking goals.

When you're satisfied with the qualities you've chosen, copy them onto the lines below. If you'd like to add a fourth to the list, go ahead (more than four is unwieldy).

My Public Speaking Avatar's Qualities, Strengths, and/or Skills

1 _____

2 _____

3 _____

4 _____

> What's In a Name? Plenty!

Congratulations—you've taken a big first step toward being your best public speaking self!

Your next step is to name your Avatar.

Since this name is private, you can go wild. Be as creative, irreverent, funny, outlandish, or cautious and conventional as you like. But pick a name that, in your own mind, stands for the best of YOU.

My Avatar's Name Is:

_____

corporate Girl

In my former career as a speechwriter and marketing communications consultant, I thought of ⋆**JEZRA**⋆ as "Corporate Girl."

Corporate Girl was poised, patient, friendly, and enthusiastic almost all the time. She wasn't "the whole truth and nothing but the truth" about me, but she was *the truth told well.*

> But Wait... I Thought I was Supposed to Speak Like *ME!*

You are. You will.

And the beauty of your Avatar, as you'll discover, is that, since he or she is the *best of you*, slipping into his or her skin will let you *easily* speak like *the best of yourself.*

You'll take your Avatar for a test drive soon. But for now, let's turn to Chapter 2 and look at what happens when people first discover that they're going to be making a speech.

Take-Away

While many people feel that they *should* speak differently, that perception comes from a nasty little self-critical voice (NLV), and not from the realities of what it takes to be a good public speaker.

In reality, speaking like *your best self* is the fastest route to success; and it starts with appreciating your existing communications strengths, skills and qualities. These will become the basis for your public speaking Avatar—a streamlined version of *the best of yourself* that can help you in every public speaking situation.

Defining and naming your Avatar is the first step toward becoming the kind of public speaker that *you* want to be.

> Chapter 2

Doomed to Fail vs. Speak Like Yourself

Why do so many speakers put their audiences to sleep?

You might think it's because they're not good speakers. But while that may be true, there's also a deeper reason:

Their **speeches** aren't good.

And those speeches *can't* be good, because they're built with a process that leads straight to mediocrity.

> You Can't Get There from Here

Pretend that your boss has just "asked" you to make a speech at an upcoming meeting or event.

You've never made a speech before—or worse, you've made a speech and it didn't go well— but that's not something you're eager to tell your boss. So you gulp and take the assignment.

What happens next? (I mean *after* the panic attack!)

Why Panic?

People who panic at the thought of public speaking are often dismissed as being too sensitive. But they've grasped an underlying truth that their hardier colleagues tend to ignore: *They don't know how to pull this off!*

They've never been taught basic speechmaking skills; so on what basis would they feel confident?

Your next move will probably be to call a trusted friend, colleague, or mentor and ask them how you should proceed.

"No problem," they're likely to tell you. "It's not that hard to put a speech together." They will then explain how they've gone about preparing to give speeches in the past, or how they've observed their own colleagues, mentors, or bosses doing it.

What they'll probably relay to you is the gold standard in business speechmaking—a simple[1], easily implemented process that I call the Doomed to Fail Approach.

Here are the three steps in Doomed to Fail:

Doomed to Fail Step 1: Find Out Everything You Can about Your Topic
Doomed to Fail Step 2: Put Your Facts into PowerPoint
Doomed to Fail Step 3: Ignore Your Speech Until the Day You Give It

Let's take a quick look at this approach, so that you understand what's wrong with it.

› Doomed to Fail Step 1: Find Our Everything You Can About Your Topic

There are two big problems with starting your speechmaking process by jumping straight into topic research:

- You don't know what will interest your audience; and
- Since you don't know what will interest your audience, you have no criteria for choosing what to tell them (in other words, for narrowing down your topic).

In fact, most people *don't* narrow down their topics. They just research everything that could possibly pertain to the title they've been given. And believe it or not, the title is *all* that most people have to work with when they begin to gather information for a speech.

If speech titles were *wonderful*... if they conveyed a unique *attitude*... if they united your expertise and your *audience's concerns*... this wouldn't be a problem.

---

[1] As the writer and social observer H.L. Mencken observed, "For every complex problem, there is an answer that's simple, clear, and wrong."

But 99% of the time, speech titles don't do any of these things.[2]

Instead, your title is likely to be a bland construction that purposefully avoids a point of view, such as:

- A Review of Phase One Findings
- Creating a High-Value Team
- Next Steps to eCommerce Implementation

Why are these titles so non-committal? Because no one wants to give a speech with a title that commits them to saying unpopular things, like:

- A Review of Phase One Findings Shows How Much Work We Still Have to Do
- Creating a High-Value Team is Probably Impossible, But We'll Try Anyway
- The Next Steps to eCommerce Implementation are Being Outsourced

Where Do Speech Titles Come From?

Having written speeches for countless corporate events, I know a lot about how this particular sausage gets made. Often, a writer, a creative director, an account executive (salesperson) and/or an event planner are sitting in a room trying to figure out how they're going to fill X days of time, and someone will say, "We need to put the VP of Marketing onstage Wednesday morning." "OK," someone else will say, "Let's give her 45 minutes and call it *Overview of Our New Marketing Materials*."

Remember that these people don't know you, nor are they concerned with your success. Their goal is to fill out a program. So take the title you're assigned with a large grain of salt, and use it as a *general suggestion* for what you should speak about, not as a set of instructions for your speech.

Even when a speech contains positive news, the general practice is to give it a vague, lackluster title.

That isn't necessarily a *bad* thing. But be sure that your bland title doesn't lead you to create a bland speech!

---

[2] You've probably noticed that 99% of the statistics I use are intended as hyperbole; or rather, they reflect my subjective experience. Please assume that, unless I quote a reliable source, any data I present is a "guestimate" that represents my humble opinion.

> Beware the Dreaded Data Dump

A vague title isn't the only reason that you should beware of jumping straight into research.

Since you don't know *specifically* what your talk with cover (or what your audience needs to hear), making a grab for whatever information you or your assistant can find—unfiltered by any criteria for relevance—can lead to the dreaded "data dump."

What's a data dump? Picture a dump truck—the kind that's used to lay a load of gravel on a driveway or other work site. (If you have a young child, this image will come easily to mind.)

But the particular truck I want you to picture isn't loaded down with gravel. Instead, it's filled with every fact, figure, book, article, piece of information, or internet reference that's even remotely connected to your topic.

Now imagine dumping all of that content onto your desk, and figuratively shoveling through it to find something worth saying.

At best, you've got a mess on your hands. And even if you had time to sort through the whole pile (which you don't), how could you possibly separate the items that are useful from the ones that should go straight to landfill?

Clearly, you can't.

> Doomed to Fail Step 2: Put Your Facts Into PowerPoint

Because it's not easy to make sense of all the information you've collected, most speakers don't even try. Instead, they go straight to Doomed to Fail Step 2, and dump their data straight into overloaded PowerPoint[3] slides.

Why are these slides overloaded?

---

[3] By "PowerPoint," I also mean Keynote, the far more intuitive PowerPoint equivalent for Macs.

Because most speakers compound the problem of having too much data by not organizing it effectively. Instead of putting just *one thought* on each slide, they put *everything they know* about *one aspect of their topic* on each slide.

Two graphs? Four pictures? Six lines of argument? No problem; if they're related, someone will put them on the same slide, and that slide may well look like this[4]:

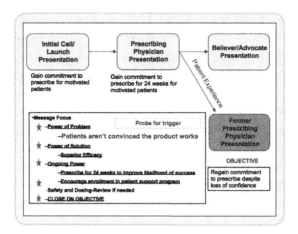

This PowerPoint, like so many that you see in business settings, has no underlying logic or story. And if the slides that proceed and follow it are equally obscure, whoever is presenting them will have to fall back on that old business standby of presenting each slide without relating it to the others.

You've heard speakers do that. They say, "What this slide shows... this next slide shows... this slide illustrates... now let's look at..."

Ho-hum.

> **Blind Men and Elephants**

Listening to someone present a series of disjointed PowerPoint slides reminds me of the parable of the Blind Men and the Elephant.

In this story, which originated in India, several blind men are trying to determine what an elephant looks like.

---

[4] This is an honest-to-goodness, real (though carefully redacted) client slide from my corporate days.

But because each one is examining a different part of its body, they reach very different, disjointed conclusions:

- The man who's patting the elephant's trunk thinks an elephant is a long, tube-like animal.
- The man who's touching the elephant's ears thinks that it's a wide, floppy, animal.
- The man who's tracing the elephant's leg thinks it's a short, stubby animal, etc.

Similarly, a series of unrelated slides don't give you the add up to a big picture. And, as a public speaker, **your job is to deliver the big picture**—to present the whole elephant, if you will.

Your job is *not* to offer the speechmaking equivalent of, "This piece is long and tube-like... this piece is wide and floppy... this piece is short and stubby."

Yawn!

› Just Tell Me What I Need to Know

In my corporate speechwriting days, I used to ask my clients a lot of "hard" questions like "What am I supposed to learn from this slide?"

And what I discovered, time after time, was that the thing my client wanted me to learn was obscured by a pile of hopelessly other data that added nothing to my understanding.

Here's an example:

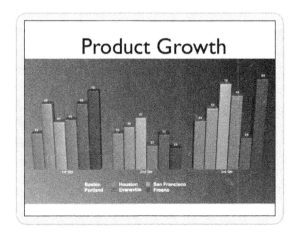

Often, when someone delivers a slide like this on, they'll say, "*As you can see*, San Francisco grew 76% in Q3."

But, of course, you *can't* see that, because by the time you figure out where the data for Q3 (the third quarter) is, let alone which bar represents San Francisco, the presenter has gone on to his or her next slide. (And you'll probably also miss the *next* data point, because you'll still be trying to decode *this* one).

So why not use a visual approach that immediately conveys what's *most important*, such as:

I'm no graphic artist, but this slide has one unassailable virtue: No one in your audience will miss the fact that San Francisco was up 76% in Q3.

You can only pull off this approach if you know what data is important to your audience. But wouldn't you want to know that anyway?

> Doomed to Fail Step 3: Ignore Your Speech Until the Day You Give It

By the time most presenters have created a PowerPoint, they're pretty sure that their speech isn't going to be great. And they're *very* sure they don't know how to change that.

So what do they do?

They put the whole damned thing out of their minds—or at least, they trying to fool themselves into thinking that's what they've done.

This is why so many presenters show up on Speech Day to deliver a talk with which they're utterly unfamiliar.

They spent minimal time writing the thing, they never practiced it, and they've done their best to ignore it ever since. Now they're going to have to *figure out* what their slides are supposed to mean—onstage, in front of hundreds of people.

> ### What *Is* This Speech About, Anyway?
>
> This is a very good self-test question. If you can't answer it clearly and succinctly, in one sentence, you're not ready to deliver this speech!

Paradoxically, the other way to ignore your speech right up to the last possible minute is to keep compulsively editing it. I once saw an executive literally making edits to her speech notes *as she was walking to the stage*.

This is the essence of Doomed To Fail; and of course her speech was terrible. How could it be otherwise, when she saw her speech as (a) a written document instead of a spoken communication, and (b) a flawed collection of words that she was neither proud of, nor ready to, present?

If you treat your speech like a *written document that isn't good enough to be shared*, it's no surprise that you won't enjoy sharing it—and that your audience won't enjoy listening.

❯ The Speak Like Yourself Approach

Doesn't the Doomed to Fail approach sound like fun?

No?

Well, here's the good news: You can start right now to replace the three Doomed to Fail steps with an approach that actually *works*.

Believe it or not, this approach is going to lead you straight to a speech that you'll *enjoy* delivering. It's also a speech that your audience will enjoy hearing, because it's crafted specifically for *them*.

The three Speak Like Yourself steps are:

Speak Like Yourself Step 1: Prepare a Speech that's Valuable to Your Audience

Speak Like Yourself Step 2: Practice Delivering It Powerfully

Speak Like Yourself Step 3: Connect with Your Listeners and Present with Pride

In the chapters that follow, you'll learn about each of these steps, and how to apply them effectively, every time.

For now, though, the thing to remember is that, unlike Doomed to Fail, which is focused entirely on your *content*, the Speak Like Yourself approach succeeds because it recognizes that public speaking is a **relationship** that also involves *people*.

Here's what that relationship looks like:

> It's Not About You!

As you can see from this illustration, there are three elements in a public speaking relationship, and you're only one of them. The other two are:

Your *audience*: a collection of people who'd like to get some value for the time they're putting in; and

Your *content*: a collection of ideas that deliver that value.

OK, It's One-Third About You!

Since you're one-third of the public speaking equation, it probably makes sense to put one-third of your attention on yourself and your experience. What doesn't make sense is to put 99% of your attention on either your content, or on concerns about you, i.e., on whether or not you'll succeed.

Like all good relationships, the one between you, your content, and your audience is fluid. It can grow stronger during the course of a speech. Here's how that works:

- **If you respect your audience** and take their needs and interests into account, they'll generally return the favor by listening to what you have to say.
- **As you notice your audience listening with respect**, you'll deliver your content more powerfully.
- **The more powerful your content sounds**, the more your audience will realize that it brings them value... and the more respect they'll have for it—and you.

Think of this as a feedback loop where everybody benefits: The more value you offer, the more your audience will listen with care. And the more carefully they listen, the more your confidence will grow.

Now, I can't promise that things will go this way absolutely *every* time.

But even when they don't work out, isn't it better to keep this model in mind than to think of your speech as a gladiator-style fight to the death in which your job is to be flawless, and the audience's job is to rip you to shreds when you're not?

> OK, I'm Convinced. What's Next?

In Chapter 1, we talked about YOU. We asked,

What are your communications strengths, skills, and qualities?
Are you willing to speak like yourself?
Would having an Avatar make that easier?

In this chapter, we've talked about YOUR CONTENT, or rather, where people go wrong when they attempt to choose content using the Doomed to Fail approach.

Now it's time to think about the third element of a public speaking relationship: YOUR AUDIENCE. Understanding them is the first step toward speechmaking success—and we'll talk about how to achieve that understanding in Chapter 3.

Take-Away

The way that most public speakers go wrong is by leaving people out of their equation. A speech that is built around a title or topic can never be as rich or persuasive as one that's built with a particular audience and their needs and interests in mind.

That's why you should avoid the Doomed to Fail approach that begins with a data dump, involves not practicing, and ends with putting your head in the sand.

Instead, in the rest of this book, you'll learn how to execute each of the three Speak Like Yourself steps: (1) prepared a speech that has value for your audience; (2) practice delivering it powerfully; and (3) connect with your listeners and present your speech with pride.

Chapter 3

Understanding Your Audience

In Chapter 2, you learned about the three steps to great speechmaking:

Speak Like Yourself Step 1: Prepare a Speech that's Valuable to Your Audience

Speak Like Yourself Step 2: Practice Delivering It Powerfully

Speak Like Yourself Step 3: Connect with Your Listeners and Present with Pride

Now we're going to focus on that first step.

> You're Not Just Talking, You're Talking to Someone

The biggest underlying assumption in this book is that the success of your speech will be determined in large part by whether you deliver value to your audience.

That's worth repeating: The success of your speech won't be determined by your smooth delivery, or your perfect word choice (though, don't get me wrong, those things are fun to pull off). It will be determined by your audience's view of whether or not *you were worth listening to.*

But before you can prepare a speech that will be of value to your audience, you have to:

- Know how a speech is actually prepared, and
- Understand what your *audience* would find valuable.

That's why, before we can talk about **how** to prepare an effective speech, we need to understand **who** you'll be preparing it for.

> **What Do You Mean by "Value"?**
>
> I mean: Anything your audience is glad to have heard.
>
> *News you can use* is valuable. Inspiration is valuable. Accurate and time-saving instructions are valuable. Information about what's going to happen is valuable. Tips and tricks can be valuable. Heart-warming stories can be valuable. Watch-outs, even reprimands can be valuable if they're done right.
>
> A full list of what comprises value would be very, very long. So it's *your* job to become the expert who understands what "value" means to your particular audience.

> Getting to Know Your Audience

You remember this illustration, right? It's the public speaking relationship we talked about in Chapter 2.

How do you create this relationship?

Start by asking some basic questions about your audience (you'll also find these questions in the Instant Speech Worksheet in Appendix A):

1. Who are they (in relation to my speech)?
2. What do I want them to do, or do differently?
3. Why should they care? (What's in it for them?)

Let's look briefly at each of these questions, and what they mean for crafting a speech:

> ### What's With All This "Relationship" Talk??
>
> OK, I admit the R-word can get tiring. We could call it a *transaction*. An *interaction*. An *exchange*. A *connection*.
>
> Or, because it's about relating to your audience and bringing content that meets their needs, you could call the public speaking relationship... a *relationship*!

> Who Are They (in Relation to My Speech)?

Imagine that you're a small manufacturer of **custom gardening tools**, and you've been invited to give a talk about your products.

The first thing you need to know is: *Who will you be talking to*? Are they:

Gardeners who belong to a local gardening club?
Crime Writers, looking for new kinds of murder weapons to feature in their novels?
Buyers for Wal*Mart's gardening department?

Each of these audiences would get a very different speech, so know which one you'll be addressing!

> What Do I Want Them To Do, or Do Differently?

This is *your* "What's in it for me?" question—and again, the answer depends on who *they* are!

Gardeners could buy your tools, and help spread the word to other potential customers.

Crime Writers could use your brand in their books' grizzly murders, and maybe even help get your products placed in the movies that are made from their books.

Buyers from Wal*Mart, can stock your tools, and sell them to a national market.

› Why Should They Care (What's In It for Them)?

Another way to ask this question is, "What benefit can I offer my audience that will persuade them to give me what I want?"

Or, in more relationship-based terms, "How can I help my audience appreciate that doing X will be good for everyone?"

Is There Such a Thing as "Win-Win" Situation?

Before the concept of "win-win" became almost as big a business cliché as the moribund "out of the box," these situation used to be called by other names: Compromise. Collaboration. Mutual interest.

I'm not suggesting that you b.s. your audience about what is or isn't to their benefit. What I suggest is that you look for the ways in which whatever you're proposing genuinely *is* to everyone's benefit, and make that case.

So what would the audience for your speech on gardening tools find of benefit—and therefore, of interest?

Gardeners will buy your tools if using them leads to better gardens. Better gardens, in turn, might bring them more happiness, pride, and/or status among gardeners.

Crime Writers will be thrilled to have their characters kill people with your tools if you can suggest some new, page-turning plot ideas.

Buyers from Wal*Mart are looking for profit, so point out that your large customer base will gladly pay premium prices for your tools, even though they're relatively cheap to produce.

See how this is done?

Asking questions about your audience will prompt you to think about how to meet *their* needs— and your own.

Once you know how to meet everyone's needs, it's a lot easier to craft a speech that will do the job.

> What If It's More Complicated?

Of course, there *are* situations in which your audience's needs may not overlap with yours, or may be difficult to meet or impossible to discern. So before we jump into *writing a speech*, let's look at some of those more complex audience scenarios:

When You're Bringing Bad News

It's not always possible to present content that will please your listeners. Sometimes you have no choice but to anger or upset your audience.

But, surprisingly, that doesn't mean that you and your audience have to be at odds.

Even if they strenuously object to, or disagree with, what you're saying, they'll still be more willing to listen to you if they feel that *you've taken them into account.*

If you show respect for their thoughts and feelings (*real* respect, not the pretend kind); if you've clearly given thought to how they'll react to what you're telling them; if you're willing to speak from a place of reality, not denial or false good cheer; then you still have a chance to connect with them, and perhaps even mitigate the pain of bad news.

> ### Up in the Air... or Out to Lunch?
>
> In the 2009 film *Up in the Air*, George Clooney played a man whose job was to convince people who were being fired that *this was a good thing for them*. Even though his goal was manipulative (to avoid scenes and law suits), he made people feel genuinely better because he listened respectfully to them, and reacted with real empathy.

In contrast, I recall a meeting, held in the lunchroom of my daughter's high school, between a representative from NYC's Department of Education and a group of parents. The parents were concerned and angry following an incident at the school, and were complaining that overcrowding made the school unsafe. To which the DOE's representative replied (and I quote), "You should be *grateful* that you're not at 150% of capacity like Fort Hamilton High." She also said that our school was overcrowded because of the DOEs larger plan, and that, "You have to break some eggs to make an omelette."

If you want to see a group of nice, working- and middle-class moms turn into a rabid mob, just suggest that you're willing to *break* our children. The DOE representative had clearly not anticipated her audience's reaction, and she left that cafeteria quick, fast, and in a hurry, before someone (probably her) got hurt.

When You're Speaking to Several Equally Important Groups

Imagine that you're a consultant who's been hired to move a start-up company from their current office to a new one. You've been asked to come in and brief people on the move.

Your audience will consist of the IT *and* sales *and* creative departments. So who among them really matters to you?

Everyone. In order for this move to go smoothly, everyone's going to have to be onboard.

You can accomplish this goal by addressing each group's specific concerns in turn, rather than by trying to talk to them all at once. Tell them that:

- The #1 concern for IT—**getting their data center up and running**— will be your team's first priority following the move.

- As soon as the network is on line, the #1 priority for Sales—**getting access to their customer information**—will be taken care of next.

- And the #1 priority for Creative—**settling into their new work space**—will be left in the hands of the Creative team, so that they can set up in the exact way they want.

Segmenting your audience in this way is much more effective than resorting to broad generalities. ("We're taking all your concerns into account.") And since you'll be speaking to each group in the room about what concerns them most, people will be more willing to wait quietly while you address the other groups.

When You're Not Sure Who the Decision-Maker Is

This happens sometimes when you're interviewing for a job, or pitching new business.

How do you know who matters most to you if you find yourself in a room with multiple people whose roles are poorly defined (or who are introduced to you hastily, or in a mumble)?

It's best to identify the decision-maker in advance. But if you're not able to do that, *look for the person that others are deferring to*—their body language should be pretty obvious—and address what you're saying to him or her.

This doesn't mean that you can ignore or belittle anyone else; you should be warm, friendly, and interested in all. But tailor your talk to the person who'll be deciding on your job application or business proposal, because he or she is your true audience.

Uncovering the Power

When the question is, "Who will be deciding on my job application (or proposal, or request for a raise, etc.)?" remember that   knows the answer. If you can find the person who has this information, ask them in a tactful way to tell you whatever they can.

There's nothing wrong with asking, "Can you give me any insights into the decision-making process?" or "Do you know who'll be making the final decision?" or "Can you help me understand how a decision will be made?"

Even if you don't get information, you'll have given it your best shot—and shown that you really care about the outcome.

When There's Nothing You Want From Your Audience

The second audience analysis question is, "What do I want the people in my audience to do, or do differently?"

Some of my clients will say, "I don't want them to do *anything* differently," "I just want to make them aware of my organization's program," or "I just want to educate them about my products."

To which I say, "Really? You don't want them to *buy* your products? You don't want them to *donate* to your program?"

If you're shy, or conflict-averse, or have a live-and-let-live attitude, you may find it hard to admit that yes, you actually *want something*. But for me, it's an article of faith that every speaker wants *something*—even if it's "just" your audience's respect and approval.

So if you *just* want your audience to know what you think, consider the possibility that you actually want them to *adopt* your thinking!

Look Out for Just

Plenty of women, as well as many men, minimize our own desires by using the word *just*, as in, "I just want them to know how hard I've been working." (Really? You mean, you don't want a *raise*?)

While *just* can appear in statements that are true ("I just got home five minutes ago"), if it's followed by a statement of what you or someone else *desires*, that statement should be considered suspect.

It's good to know what you want from your audience. Knowing what you want will make your speech more authentic, and will bring you closer to getting the desired result.

In Chapter 4, we'll look at the role your Key Message plays in making that happen.

Take-Away

Public speaking success is based on your audience's perception that you've delivered value on their terms. To do this, you must know who you're talking to, and what they want.

You also need to know what you want from them. Armed with this knowledge, you can look for areas in which your audience's needs and your own needs overlap.

Even in difficult situations, you can succeed if you've thought about your audience. Ask yourself: "Who are they (in relation to my speech)?" "What do I want them to do, or do differently?" and "Why should they care (what's in it for them)?"

> Chapter 4

Your Key Message a/k/a "The Big Key"

In Chapter 3, we talked about how to figure out who's in your audience, what you want them to do differently, and what's in it for them.

Now you're ready for **Speak Like Yourself Step 1: Prepare a Speech that's Valuable to Your Audience**. And the good news is, that's not as hard as it may sound.

In fact, you'll be doing *70% of your speechwriting work*[5] when you create just one sentence: your Key Message.

> When You Don't Know What to Say

Many people go completely blank when they have to give a presentation, or even an opinion at work; or when they're asked to "say a few words" at a social function like a wedding.

There are personal reasons for the blank-out, and we'll discuss some of them in Chapter 11, on Public Speaking Panic.But there's also a simple and logical reason why people feel tongue-tied at these moments: *They truly don't know what to say!*

There are so many different things you could talk about, so many possible comments to make. How do you decide which one(s) to choose? How do you even know where to start?

[5] Yes, 70% is arbitrary. This figure illustrates my own experience with Key Messages, which is that, with the right one, everything else in a speech falls into place. (It's also my experience that with a weak, or absent, Key Message, the speech just won't come together optimally, no matter how hard I work on it.)

Here's where:

Start your thinking about every presentation—whether it's going to be a major speech to 5000 people, or a short statement at your work team's weekly meeting—by identifying the *core* of what you want to say.

That core idea, known as your **Key Message**, is truly *the big key* to public speaking success.

› What *Is* a Key Message?

At its simplest, your Key Message is *the biggest, most truc, and most important thing you have to say about any given topic.*

Your Key Message is literally the point that your speech is setting out to prove. It also:

- Begins your speech;
- Ends your speech; and
- Determines how you'll organize everything else in your speech.

That's a lot for one sentence to accomplish—but your Key Message, a/k/a The Big Key, does even more! It opens the door to:

- An easy speechmaking process;
- A successful presentation; and
- A positive reaction from your audience.

How does your Key Message succeed at all these tasks?

By bringing your interests (what you want) and the interests of your audience (what they want) together in one idea—thereby supporting the public speaking relationship that we discussed in Chapters 2 and 3.

On the next page, you'll find examples of what that can sound like. (As with all the examples in this book, read them out loud to get the full effect.)

Your Interest	Your Audience's Interest	Key Message
Selling children's car seats ("Buy my company's car seat.")	Keeping their children safe when they travel by car ("I want to buy the safest car seat on the market.")	"My company's car seats have won Consumer Reports' top rating for child safety, in each of the past five years—and for good reason."
Raising money for cancer research ("Please donate.")	Knowing that their donations are being spent effectively ("Don't waste my hard-earned dollars.")	"The funds that you've so generously invested will change millions of people's lives—and tonight, I'm going to explain why we're so sure of that fact."
Getting hired as a project manager ("Hire me.")	Hiring a great project manager ("Why should I?!")	"I would love to work for you. And I truly believe that my experience and qualifications are perfect for your needs."

› Your Key Message Is What People Will Remember

In addition to being the most important idea in your speech, your Key Message is likely to be the **only** thing that people remember.

If you doubt this, think about how much you remember from the last speech you heard. Do you recall the:

- Speech's title?
- Facts and examples that were used?
- Graphs and charts that were presented?
- Detailed arguments that were made?

Probably not.

You might recall a vivid or moving story, or a general line of thought. But if you can repeat *one thing* that you heard a speaker say, it probably was their Key Message.

That's why your Key Message should be the *biggest*, *most true*, and *most important* thing you have to say.

Since it's all your audience is likely to remember, you don't want to waste it!

› A Key Message Needs Personality

In addition to being *big*, *true* for the person who's speaking, and important for both speaker and audience, a good Key Message has *personality*. It leave you in no doubt about the speaker's point of view.

Agree or disagree with it, a good Key Message grabs you (sometimes, by the throat!) and makes you pay attention to what follows.

Here are some Key Messages that accomplish that goal:

"No dying person has ever said that he wished he'd spent more time in the office."

"Unless we reorganize this company, we're headed for a crash-and-burn."

"We should sell our house and move to the country."

"The only way to save this economy is by supporting local small businesses."

"Jimi Hendrix was the most important guitar player in history."

"Women should not serve in military combat units."

"We've almost reached the point of no return with global warming."

"It doesn't matter who's President; the same wealthy people will still run the show."

"Children who don't have siblings are smarter than children who do."

"The best thing that ever happened to space exploration is private investment."

"America is a Christian country."

In contrast, these messages, like the Doomed to Fail speech titles in Chapter 2, are not compelling because they have no personality and very little point of view:

> "We are facing an important challenge."
>
> "I take full responsibility for what happened."
>
> "We performed above expectation."
>
> "Everyone is required to meet the sales goal."

› What If Your Key Message Doesn't Have a Big Personality?

That's OK.

I just said that your Key Message needs a *personality*—and it does. But that personality can be sincere, modest, even understated, as long as what you're saying matters.

Here are some humble Key Messages that probably sounded very big to the people who heard them:'

> "I can solve your problem."
>
> "You did a great job on this assignment."
>
> "We've made our decision, and the promotion is yours."
>
> "Thank you!"

The Best Key Message of All

Do you remember the first time your partner, your child, or someone else who means the world to you said, "I love you"?

Not particularly original, right? But could there be a sweeter, more satisfying Key Message? "I love you" might be the biggest Big Key ever—and there's nothing unique or clever about it!

> Is Every Key Message a "Big Key"?

With so much riding on your Key Message, how do you know you've found a true Big Key—one that unlocks the full potential of your speech?

Here are two questions that will quickly reveal whether your Key Message is big, true, important, and memorable enough to carry an entire presentation.

Think of them as **The Key to the Key**:

1. If this Key Message is *the only thing* my audience remembers, have I made my point?
2. If my audience believes that this Key Message is true, am I closer to getting what I want?

The following true story illustrates how useful these two questions can be, particularly when feelings are running high.

My Daughter and the Subway, Part 1

When my daughter was 16, she called one night to say that she wouldn't be home by her midnight curfew because she was halfway across town and couldn't find a cab to bring her back. Her plan was to hop on the subway *(alone, at midnight!)*, and be half an hour late. This gave me 30 minutes to think about what I was going to say to her when she finally arrived home.

When I'm giving a workshop or seminar, I often ask the participants what they would have said in my situation; and people come up with Key Messages like these:

"How could you do this to me?"
"Don't you realize it's dangerous out there?"
"You could have been raped! You could have been robbed!"
"I'm very angry at you."

These are all valid messages, but they don't pass the two **Key to the Key** tests. That's because, if these messages were the only thing my daughter remembered me saying to her, I wouldn't be closer to getting what I wanted, even if she believed they were true.

Once I realized *what I wanted*, I knew that my Key Message should be, **"You will never again take the subway home alone at midnight."** This message passed both tests, and—with the help of Supporting Points that you'll learn about in Chapter 5— it also persuaded my daughter, for at least six months!

> Watch Out for Too Much Tact

In addition to being a good example of how you can test your Key Message, the story about my daughter and the subway also illustrates the value of saying exactly what you mean.

While simplicity and understatement are fine for Key Messages, having a mushy meaning is not. So don't let a desire to be kind or tactful obscure what your Key Message *really* needs to say.

Tact is often—though not exclusively—a woman's challenge. Many women believe that being direct isn't feminine; so we try to influence others by *implying* what we want instead of *stating* it.

- Tactful Comment: "Do you want to lead the update meeting?" (Translation: "I want you to lead the update meeting.")
- Tactful Comment: "It would be great if I could have the report by Monday."(Translation: "Your deadline is Monday.")
- Tactful Comment: "Mr. Big is an important client." (Translation: "So make his account your top priority.")

If these "tactful comments" sound like you, consider toughening up your Key Messages. Remember that, while it's great for an audience to like you, it's also important for them to *get your point.*

> Small Words, Big Changes

Another way to unintentionally water down the impact of a Key Message is to not pay attention to little words. The following Key Messages differ by just *one word*. Yet they have very different implications, and would lead to very different types of speeches:

Key Message 1: We must launch our new product by June. (Implication: "We'll be in trouble if we don't.")

Key Message 2: We hope to launch our new product by June. (Implication: "But it's possible that we won't be ready.")

Key Message 3: We will launch our new product by June. (Implication: "So I expect everyone to do his or her part.")

You can see that the words *must, hope,* and *will* create a world of difference in the message's meaning:

Key Message 1 ("must launch") attempts to motivate people to join an effort, with an implied threat about what will happen if they don't.

Key Message 2 ("hope to launch") is preparing them for an uncertain future, with an implied request that they stay flexible.

Key Message 3 ("will launch") is stating a fact. The launch is set, so it's time for everyone to get onboard.

You can see, from these examples, how easy it would be to choose a Key Message that isn't quite what you mean, and end up with a speech that doesn't quite serve your needs.

Conversely, if you pick your Key Message with care, and test it using The Key to the Key, your audience will understand exactly what you want from them, and you'll be much more likely to get it.

In Chapter 5, you'll tackle the next step in the process, turning your Key Message into an Instant Speech.

Take-Away

Your Key Message (a/k/a The Big Key) is the core points of any communication, large or small. It should be big, true, important, have personality, and relate your interests to those of your audience members.

Test your message by asking, "If this is the only thing my audience remembers, have I made my point?" and "If my audience believes that this Key Message is true, am I closer to getting what I want?"

If the answers to both questions are yes, you're well on your way to creating a speech.

> Chapter 5

Turn Your Key Message into an Instant Speech

In Chapter 4, you learned how to create a Key Message that supports your relationship with your audience, gets your point across, and moves you closer to getting what you want by also addressing what *your audience* wants (what's in it for them).

The next step in developing your public speaking skills is to turn your Key Message into an **Instant Speech**.

> The Glorious, Versatile Instant Speech!

What is an Instant Speech? It's a fast and reliable way to:

- Organize your thoughts;
- Express them persuasively; and
- Sound good doing it!

The Instant Speech is simple to create and fun to deliver. It pulls your listeners along, drawing them gently toward your conclusion. It's also the basis for longer, more formal, or more elaborate presentations. And best of all, when you're delivering an Instant Speech, you always know exactly where you are, where you're going, and how you're going to get there.

In fact, an Instant Speech will help you handle most of the communications challenges you face, including:

Job interviews	Brief presentations
Pitches	Long presentations
Negotiations	Media interviews
Off-the-cuff remarks	Q&A

But don't think of the Instant Speech as just a means to an end. It's an elegant, effective format that deserves respect in its own right.

So what is this magical Instant Speech format?

> Brackets and Buckets

An Instant Speech is basically a collection of verbal **brackets** and **buckets**.

First, the brackets:

 Think of your Key Message as forming two **brackets** that hold the rest of your speech in place. Since your Key Message is the most important thing your audience will hear, it should be both the first and the last substantive thing you tell them.

In between the Key Message brackets, your speech contains three equal-sized **buckets**. (If you'd rather imagine containers or coffee cups, please do!)

These buckets contain your **Supporting Points**—the information, anecdotes, arguments, and more—that you'll use to explain, expand upon, and prove the value of your Key Message.

Supporting Points come in lots of shapes and sizes. They can be long or short. Simple or complex. Factual or theatrical. And they can be presented in myriad forms, such as:

Facts	Questions	Comments
Figures	Quotations	Instructions
Stories	Arguments	Observations
Studies	Anecdotes	Jokes

Although many speakers fall back on bar graphs and pie charts to illustrate their Supporting Points, this is an area where you have more choice than might at first be obvious.

So, for example:

- If you're talking about results from the U.S. Census, you might cite facts and figures. But you could also tell stories about "average" Americans, or show pictures that illustrate how culturally different two neighboring Census tracts can be

- If you're speaking about the safety of nuclear power, you might give statistics about the Fukashima and Chernobyl disasters; but you could also show an animation that explains the half-life of nuclear material. Or you could show a clip from *The Day After*, a 1980's TV movie about a nuclear attack on Lawrence, Kansas, and ask your audience if they think that could ever happen.

- If you're giving a presentation on how older employers can more effectively supervise young workers, you could fill your buckets with statistics. You could sample the music enjoyed by each generation in the workplace. Or you might decide to tell three stories that introduce your three Supporting Points, such as:

  - A 57-year-old boss thought she was being ignored by her young assistant—because she didn't realize he'd texted answers to her urgent questions (how different generations use technology)

  - A 23-year-old salesperson spoke so quickly that his middle-aged prospects didn't understand his pitch (how they communicate)

  - A youthful team would only make decisions by consensus, to the despair of their 45-year-old supervisor (how they prefer to interact)

As you can see, Supporting Points are endlessly flexible. But if they're so flexible (you may be wondering), why do I always group them in **three's**?

> The Rule of Three

The Rule of Three isn't really a rule (who would enforce it?). It's actually an acknowledgement that anything that comes in three's has a built-in fascination for most of the people you'll be speaking to.

If you listen to people who speak well, you'll hear them using The Rule of Three. They may repeat something three times. They may tell three stories. They may use three points to support an argument. (I used three examples in this paragraph, and I've done so throughout this book.)

Once you start noticing, you'll hear The Rule of Three working in countless popular and literary phrases. Read these out loud to hear the rhythm of three:

- Yesterday, today, and tomorrow
- Beginning, middle, and end
- Too big, too little, and just right (remember Goldilocks?)
- Love, honor, and cherish (traditional marriage vows)
- Father, Son, and Holy Ghost (the Christian Trinity)
- Faith, Hope, and Charity (three Greek Orthodox Saints; also three sisters who went to elementary school with me)
- Government of the people, by the people, for the people (Abraham Lincoln, in the Gettysburg Address)
- "I came, I saw, I conquered" (or, as Julius Caeser said in Latin, "Veni, vidi, vici")

You don't have to be an English major to feel the power of these phrases. Their rhythm carries listeners along, and gives your ideas a polished sound.

Is the Rule of Three Universal?

I don't know. If I were speaking in a different country, I would discuss this with a knowledgeable friend or colleague. But The Rule of Three seems to strike a universal chord in the U.S., and the way people respond to it feels like something that could be hard-wired.

> What's Wrong with Having Two or Four Supporting Points?

Nothing.

An Instant Speech with two or four buckets has its own rhythm and sense of balance. The popular and literary phrases on the next page will help you hear what that rhythm is.

Phrases with Two	Phrases with Four
Now and then	Earth, wind, fire, and water
Love and marriage	Blood, toil, tears, and sweat
Right and wrong	(coined by Winston Churchill)
Do or die	North, south, east, and west
No pain, no gain	Up, down, over, and under

Even though these phrases sound good—very good!—I'm still partial to The Rule of Three. For me, it has an intrinsic sense of seriousness and balance that's not too much, not too little, but just right for my public speaking style.

As my husband likes to say, though, "Your mileage may vary."

So if you find, as some of my public speaking clients do, that you feel most natural creating Instant Speeches with two or four buckets, go with what feels right to you.

In fact, the only way to go wrong in choosing two, three, or four Supporting Points is if you change your mind in mid-speech:

- If you start out delivering two Supporting Points, and follow through, you'll sound good.
- Ditto with three Supporting Points, or four.
- But if you start out delivering two Supporting Points and then hastily decide to add a third, your rhythm will be wrong and your speech will sound unbalance (and therefore less convincing).

So whether you feel that two, three, or four Supporting Points are best for a particular speech, don't second-guess yourself. Pick the number you think will work, and stick with it.

Why There's No "Rule of One"

Remember that old parental stand-by, "Because I said so?" This was given as a reason for you to do anything the adults didn't want to take the time to explain.

Unfortunately, when you use only one supporting point, you're in danger of sounding like a parent, as in:

Audience: Why is your Key Message true?
Speaker: Because I said so.

This may go over with toddlers, but with audiences? Not so much.

> Brackets + Buckets = Instant Speech!

OK, we know that an Instant Speech has two brackets or key messages (one at the beginning and one at the end), and, in keeping with the Rule of Three, three buckets that hold your Supporting Points.

You can short-hand that for easy recall as either:

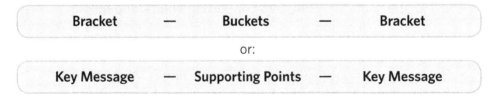

| Bracket | — | Buckets | — | Bracket |
or:
| Key Message | — | Supporting Points | — | Key Message |

In either case, here's a picture of what an Instant Speech looks like:

And here are some examples of what an Instant Speech *sounds like* (read them out loud to get the full effect).

> ## Instant Speech Example #1:
> Why Ice Cream is the Perfect Food
>
> KM: **Ice cream is the perfect food, and here's why:**
> SP: It's loaded with vitamins and minerals;
> SP: It comes in 437 flavors; and
> SP: "I scream, you scream, we all scream for ice cream."
> KM: For all of these reasons, you'd have to agree that **ice cream is the perfect food.**

OK, I'm famously addicted to ice cream. But even though the Ice Cream example is loaded with ridiculous claims, you may have noticed that its Instant Speech *rhythm* still manages to convey a certain credibility.

This example presents the Speak Like Yourself Success Steps that you learned about in Chapter 2:

> ## Instant Speech Example #2:
> Can Anyone Become a Great Public Speaker?
>
> KM: **Yes! *Anyone* can develop their public speaking strengths and skills by following these three Speak Like Yourself steps:**
> SP: First, prepare a speech that's valuable to your audience.
> SP: Then, practice delivering it powerfully. And finally,
> SP: Connect with your listeners, and present your speech with pride!
> KM: **By following these three simple Speak Like Yourself steps, *anyone* can develop their public speaking strengths and skills— and become a good, or even a *great*, public speaker!**

Finally, this real-life example completes the story about My Daughter on the Subway that began in Chapter 4. You may recall that, in this situation, my challenge was to craft a speech to give to my then 16-year-old daughter when she came home alone on the subway after midnight.

After choosing my key message ("You will never do that again!"), my next job was to choose three points to support that message and convince my daughter that I was serious.

In other words, I had three buckets to fill.

- Terrible things that could have happened?
- Examples of how angry I was?
- Advice for how she could have gotten home without having to resort to the subway?

It didn't seem likely that any of these would sell my daughter on my key message, so instead, I organized my buckets around the three people in our family.

This is the Instant Speech that resulted:

Instant Speech Example:
My Daughter on the Subway

KM: OK, listen up! **You will never again come home alone on the subway at midnight**, because, if you do:
SP: Your **Dad** will ground you for the rest of your life;
SP: Your **Mom** will embarrass you by calling every friend you've got and telling them to go out and look for you; and
SP: **You** will lose the privileges that you currently enjoy.
KM: So for all those reasons, **you will never again come home alone on the subway at midnight**. Do I have your agreement on that?

A few things about this last example:

- First (this is a wonky note), did you see that I mentioned "your Mom"? Obviously, her Mom is *me*, but I chose to go with the parallel sounding "your Dad, your Mom, and you" rather than the equally accurate, "your Dad, I, and you."
- And more importantly, I *asked for something* (her agreement) at the end of this speech.

Asking for what you want is good, because that raises the chances of you getting it. And in this case, I *did* get it; my daughter straightened up for *months*. (Don't laugh unless you've raised a teenager!)

My use of an Instant Speech to make this case also had an unintended consequence, which is that, a year later, my daughter used an Instant Speech to argue for staying out all night after Senior Prom. (*Her* ask was, "Would you please talk to Dad about this?")

And though the three examples above cover very different topics—from ice cream to public speaking to "managing" a teenager—they each have a built-in sense of balance that conveys authority and professionalism.

That's the power of Instant Speeches.

› Instant Speech Meets Job Interview

I mentioned earlier that Instant Speeches are great for job interviews.

Lots of people are interviewing these days, so let me show you what I mean (and to find out how to practice for job interviews, see Chapter 9):

Imagine that you're a project manager. You're an expert in getting things organized and done—but there are lots of people with that skill looking for work in today's market.

Before I show you how the Instant Speech format can reinforce your skills and your seriousness, let's look at how job interviews typically go:

> **Interviewer:** Can you tell me about a time when you overcame a challenge on the job?
>
> **Applicant:** Well, I guess when I supervised the Johnson account. The client was picky, but in the end they were happy with what we did.

This isn't a *bad* answer, but it's not going to help you stand out. It doesn't tell the interviewer what you did to solve the problem, or what those skills will mean for his company, if they chose to hire you.

To ace this question, prepare your answer in advance, using the approach outlined in the last few chapters, and the **Instant Speech Worksheet** in Appendix A.

Start by asking the Audience Analysis Questions from Chapter 3. Here they are, along with possible answers:

> **1.** Who are they (in relation to my speech)?
>
> *They represent the company that's considering hiring me. Their first concern, therefore, is not what I've done **before**, but what I can do for their company **now**.*

2. What do I want them to do, or do differently?

Hire me!

3. Why should they care? (What's in it for them?)

They will hire me if they believe I'm best for the job. So this question is an opportunity for me to show them how my skills and experience will apply to their company.

With that in mind, let's create an Instant Speech—a Key Message that satisfies our two Key to the Key questions from Chapter 4, plus three Supporting Points that illustrate—that answers the interviewer's question.

Interviewer: Can you tell me about a time when you overcame a challenge on the job?

Applicant: Sure, I'll tell you about the Johnson project. It was a challenge because the client didn't know what he wanted. He kept changing his mind, and the worst thing was, he was abusive to my staff.

But **(KM) we were still able to succeed because I was proactive about every aspect of the project.**

What I did was, first, **(SP1)** I made an extra effort to get to know the client, so that he always felt he could call on me. This helped protect my staff from his bad attitude.

Then **(SP2)** instead of giving him the usual three-to-four design options, I got permission to give him just one. I know that was unusual, but my manager agreed that this was a guy who would just take advantage of us if we didn't set boundaries.

And finally, **(SP3)** when it came to the review process, I made sure that some of this guy's own higher-ups were in the room. He didn't want to look silly in front of them, so he acted more decisively than if it had just been him making the call.

The result was that we were finally able to get him to sign off on a design instead of dragging things out forever. And I think **(KM) that happened because I was proactive about every aspect of the project.**

Will the interviewer by impressed by this person? I think so.

And *is this a speech you can toss off the top of your head* in the moment, under pressure?

No! Which is why, when the stakes are high, you'll want to prepare, practice, and drill your Instant Speeches in advance. (More about that in Chapters 8 and 9.)

It's Called "Editing"

I re-wrote the Instant Speech examples in this chapter several times as I was putting the book together—and then I tweaked (edited) them each a few times more. Yet some people think they "should" be able to tell a complex story smoothly, the first time they try. If *you* think this, please revisit Chapter 1!

› How to Create Supporting Point *Patterns*

You've probably noticed that I'm big on using patterns in speechmaking. Following a pattern means that your audience develops an *expectation* of what's going to happen next—and the more you fulfill that expectation, the more comfortable they'll feel with you.

One of the places where patterns work most strongly in this way is with Supporting Points:

- In the job interview example above, the *three Supporting Points describe three actions that the speaker took* to manage a difficult client. At least two of those (getting to know the client, and limiting his design choices) probably happened at the same time, but that isn't the only way that Supporting Points can *go together*.

- For instance, in the earlier example about Instant Speeches, the three Supporting Points *build on each other*, because each step must follow the one that came before it.

- And, paradoxically, in my Instant Speech about ice cream, the three Supporting Points *go together* because they're all equally *random*. (One is about fake nutrition; one is about the variety of ice cream flavors; and one is a lyric that my grandfather used to sing.)

As these examples demonstrate, Supporting Points can work together by (a) *going together*, (b) *building on each other*, or (c) counter-intuitively, by *being random*.

Here's a little more detail on each choice:

When Supporting Points Go Together

If you set up the expectation that your three Supporting Points all *go together*, you need to fulfill that expectation, as these examples do:

- apple, orange, banana
- car, truck, bus
- Canada, Mexico, the United States
- the impact of our new computer system on IT, sales, and creative
- census results from 1990, 2000, and 2010

I like to illustrate this "going togetherness" with three cards from SET®, a family card game that I highly recommend:[6]

When Supporting Points Build On Each Other

These groupings illustrate Supporting Points that *build on each other* by building in significance (or urgency, or amount), from first to last:

- The numbers 10, 10,000 and 10,000,000
- The psychology of children, teenagers, and adults
- The benefits of local investing on this town, this state, and our country
- The Olympic athletes who won bronze, silver, and gold

An illustration of this point with SET® cards would look like this:

When Supporting Points are Random

If your audience expects your Supporting Points to be unrelated, you want to fulfill that expectation, as well. Choose items that are really different, such as:

- brick, shoe, toaster oven
- Mars Rover, balloon, Vogue magazine
- computer, garden, dinosaur
- history or our company, second quarter sales results, diversity on the Board of Directors
- geography of Spain, geology of the Pleistocene Period, smart phone technology

These three cards have nothing in common, except that they're SET® cards—and that's enough:

The trick to giving a speech that has random Supporting Points is to *let your audience know that's your game plan*. ("I'm going to share three totally different ways of looking at this topic.") This lets your audience know they can relax and just go along for the ride, instead of wasting their energy looking for commonalities between your Supporting Points that aren't there.

> The One Thing You Can't Do With Supporting Points

Here's the downside of using patterns: If you start out with two Supporting Points that either go together, build on each other, or seem random—and then you *switch* the pattern—you'll unsettle your audience and make them wonder if they should be trusting you.

On the following page, you'll find some examples of bait-and-switch groupings, along with SET® cards illustrations.

Go Together, Go Together, Oops!

- apple, orange, Canada
- car, truck, census results from 2010
- the impact of our new computer system on IT, the impact of our new computer system on sales, and American foreign policy in Syria

Thing, Random Thing, First Thing?

- shoe, brick, sandal
- farm, computer, ranch
- Spain, pre-history, France

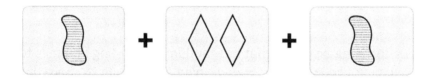

See how *clunky* things feel when your expectations aren't met?

If *you* can feel that clunk, your audience will, too—which is why The SET® Rule is so valuable.

> Be Sure to End With Your Key Message

No matter how many buckets are in your Instant Speech, and no matter how you organize your Supporting Points, **be sure that you end by repeating your Key Message.**

Repeating your Key Message can feel awkward at first ("I already said that!"), but consider this:

You want your Key Message to be the thing that people remember. And that's much more likely to happen if *it's the last thing your audience hears.*

Ending with your Key Message is also the best way to:

- Complete the Instant Speech effect of giving your words polish and authority;
- Make your Key Message even more persuasive; and
- Leave your audience with a sense of closure and satisfaction that they'll appreciate.

It also fulfills the public speaking dictum that you should *tell them what you're going to tell them* (Key Message)... *tell them* (Supporting Points)... and *tell them what you've told them* (Key Message).

So whether you think of it as *the final bracket,* or as the *second Key Message,* don't short-change that last Key Message.

It's the icing on your Instant Speech cake!

Take-Away

It's easy to turn your Key Message into an Instant Speech that will serve you in situations like job interviews, as well as presentations. To do this, add two, three, or four Supporting Points ("buckets") to your Key Message.

These Supporting Points should meet audience expectations by going together, building on each other, or being random.

And don't forget to "bracket" them by repeating your Key Message at the end of your Instant Speech. Doing so will create a balanced and authoritative presentation that sounds professional, and will ensure that your most important point is the last thing your audience hears.

> Chapter 6

Grow Your Instant Speech Into a Full-Length Presentation

In Chapters 4 and 5, you learned how to use brackets and buckets (Key Messages and Supporting Points) to create an Instant Speech.

You also learned that the Instant Speech is your go-to format for many—perhaps, most— communications challenges.

But what if you need something more substantive? How do you grow your Instant Speech into a full-length, or more detailed, presentation?

It's easy. You just:

- Bulk up (expand) your Supporting Points by adding more detail (or even, as you'll see below, by putting "buckets in your buckets"); and
- Add four brief new sections, to round out the experience.

> Supporting Points Can Be *Any* Length

It may seem hard to believe that a five-sentence Instant Speech can grow into a half-hour (or longer) presentation, but it can—through the magic of Supporting Points.

Do you remember this example of an Instant Speech from Chapter 5?

> **INSTANT SPEECH EXAMPLE:**
> Can Anyone Become a Great Public Speaker?
>
> KM: **Yes!** *Anyone* **can develop their public speaking strengths and skills by following these three Speak Like Yourself steps:**
> SP: First, prepare a speech that's valuable to your audience.
> SP: Then, practice delivering it powerfully. And finally,
> SP: Connect with your listeners, and present your speech with pride!
> KM: **By following these three simple Speak Like Yourself steps,** *anyone* **can develop their public speaking strengths and skills— and become a good, or even a** *great*, **public speaker!**

Do you remember this example of an Instant Speech from Chapter 5?

This Instant Speech has just five sentences, but I could easily expand those sentences into a discussion that lasts for 10 minutes, or 60 minutes—or the length of an entire book, like the one you're reading!

That's how it is with Supporting Points. Once you have them (and, of course, a good Key Message), you'll be surprised at how easy it is to come up with much more detailed speeches, of whatever length you need them to be.

Here's how to do that math:

- If you want to give a 30-minute speech, you have roughly seven minutes for each Supporting Point. (The rest of your time is for the other sections that you'll be learning about in this chapter.)
- If you want to give a 45-minute speech, you have roughly 12 minutes for each Supporting Point.
- If you want to give a 60-minute speech, you have roughly 17 minutes for each Supporting Point.

Doing the research and thinking that lets you fill up those buckets isn't hard for most people. (As we've seen, staying focused and organized is usually a much bigger problem.)

But what about your audience? How can you help *them* stay on track for a 17-minute Supporting Point discussion?

You do it by *sub-dividing your Supporting Points.*

> Put Buckets in Your Buckets

If I wanted to give a speech about my home town, Brooklyn New York, one of my Supporting Points might well be about the Brooklyn Bridge.

Now I *could* just talk for seven, 12, or 17 minutes about the Brooklyn Bridge. But wouldn't it be easier on everyone (meaning, both me and my listeners) if this Supporting Point was organized into a little mini-Instant Speech with brackets and buckets of its own?

Here's what doing that might sound like:

> **KM:** **The Brooklyn Bridge was an architectural breakthrough from the start; and today, it's still one of the most exciting landmarks in the country.**
>
> **SP1:** When it was completed in 1883, it was the longest suspension bridge in the world—50% longer than its nearest competitor.
>
> **SP2:** The bridge has such romantic and historical interest that it was the subject of the first PBS documentary ever made by noted filmmaker Ken Burns.
>
> **SP3:** And today, it still plays a vital role in connecting Manhattan and Brooklyn, with more than 125,000 crossings every day.
>
> **KM:** **These are just a few examples of how the Brooklyn Bridge, which began life as an architectural breakthrough, is still one of the most exciting landmarks in the country.**

This little Instant Speech works at five sentences. But I could also talk about each supporting point for five *minutes*—and presto, I would have a 17-minute Supporting Point to join two other Points about Brooklyn.

I'll also have a speech that's easy to deliver, and easy to follow.

That's because, when you divide a Supporting Point into its own brackets and buckets, both you and the audience will always know where you are in the speech, and what's likely to come next.

› Four New Speech Elements

Longer Supporting Points are critical for expanding an Instant Speech into a full-length presentation—but they're not the whole story.
To make a longer speech run smoothly, you also have to add four new elements. In order of their appearance in a speech, these elements are:

Attention Grabber: something short that focuses the audience on your topic

Preview: an overview, before the fact, of what your Supporting Points will be

Recap: a quick review, after you've delivered them, of what your Supporting Points covered

Close: the ending of your speech, which often involves asking the audience to do something about what they've just learned.

Let's look at what each of these new elements does, why you need it, and what it sounds like in a longer version of my speech about the Speak Like Yourself steps.

Attention Grabber

What's an Attention Grabber? Well, it's *not* an "Introduction."

Here's what an **Introduction** sounds like:

- "Today, I'm going to speak with you about the importance of education."
- "My topic today is our relationship with China."
- "It's a pleasure to be here to think with you about how we can boost the profits of our company."

All of those statements introduce the topic of your speech (we discussed topics and speech titles in Chapter 2), but they don't *grab the audience's attention.*

Your Attention Grabber is also not an announcement (these are sometimes called "Housekeeping").

Here's what **Housekeeping** sounds like:

- "I want to thank today's organizers for inviting me to speak."
- "Before I begin, let's have another round of applause for Jane Smith, who just spoke."
- "I've been asked to tell you that, following my speech, there'll be a 30-minute break, with refreshments served out in the hallway."
- "At the end of this presentation, I hope that you'll all fill out the evaluation form that you found under your seats."

These are all legitimate things to say, but they have nothing to do with your speech, and they certainly won't *grab your audience's attention.*

Think Carefully About Doing Housekeeping

Unless you're the event organizer as well as a speaker, Housekeeping isn't part of your job. There are reasons why you might agree to deliver some Housekeeping before your speech. These range from politics to expediency to giving yourself something trivial to say when you first get onstage and are collecting yourself.

But in a formal setting or one where you're introduced as an expert, making announcements that anyone could make may dilute your credibility (especially if you're a woman); so consider politely refusing these requests.

If You Do Pick Up the Broom

Dire warnings aside, if you do consent to do a little housekeeping, here's how to pull it off:

1. Deliver the Housekeeping announcement(s).
2. Pause for a LONG TIME, to put distance between yourself and that person who just pointed out the fire exits.
3. Then deliver your Attention Grabber *as if it's the very first thing to come out of your mouth.*

Your Attention Grabber: Now You *Can* Be Clever!

There are places in your speech—the Preview, Supporting Points, and Recap come to mind—where you're better off being serviceable than clever. The meaty middle section of your speech is not the time to dazzle your audience; it's the time to make it *easy for them to understand you.*

But the Attention Grabber is your time to shine. Here, cleverness or originality are welcome, because your goal is to *startle your audience into paying attention.*

In addition, the Attention Grabber is the first substantive thing the audience will hear you say. A surprising or intriguing Attention Grabber will let them know that they're in for a treat—*and* get your speech off to a strong start.

What *Is* a Good Attention Grabber?

You'll see from the Instant Speech Worksheet in Appendix A that your Attention Grabber is the *last* thing you write when you're putting a speech together (because you can't set up your speech until you know what's *in* your speech).

But since it's the first thing you *deliver* when you give your speech, we'll cover it first here:

As with Supporting Points, you can pick almost any form or format that you want for your Attention Grabber. The most common types of Attention Grabbers are stories, because stories have the power to immediately engage your audience's curiosity and empathy. But questions, surprising statistics, provocative quotes, and many other types of Attention Grabbers are also very effective.

The only rules are that your Attention Grabber *relate to the content of your speech* (specifically to your Key Message), and be genuinely intriguing to *you* (which ups the chance that it will be for your audience, too).

Here are some examples of Attention Grabbers—and then we'll look at how they roll into their related Key Messages.

- "How many of you expect to retire at 60?"

- "Do you know what percent of your investment dollars are put to work in your own community? (Pause... pause... pause) That percent is: ZERO!"

- "About one person in eight has the kind of fear of public speaking that gets you a medical diagnosis. (Pause) The rest of us are just plain scared."

Why All the Pauses?

Pauses are important throughout a speech, but nowhere more than at the beginning, when you're trying to *win your audience's attention.* The pause allows you to check in, to see if they're following you, and to create a little drama that makes your statement even more intriguing. It also gives your audience time to get used to hearing the sound of your voice, while you get used to being on stage and connecting with the people you're speaking to.

When you put them with their respective and related Key Message, here's what you get:

- "How many of you expect to retire at 60? (Pause) Apparently not very many. (Pause) That's why I'm so excited to tell you that, in the next few years, *some great new employment and career opportunities will become available to older adults.*"

- "Do you know what percentage of your investment dollars are put to work in your own community? (Pause... pause... pause) ZERO! So, in the next few minutes, we're going to look at how we can change that. Because *putting even 1% of your investment dollars into local small businesses would be enough to fix the economy in this community... in our country... and perhaps in the whole world.*"

- "About one person in eight has the kind of fear of public speaking that gets you a medical diagnosis. (Pause) The rest of us are just plain scared. But that fear tends to diminish when you realize that *anyone can develop their public speaking strengths and skills by following the three Speak Like Yourself steps to great public speaking.*"

You've now delivered your Attention Grabber and Key Message.

Next comes...

› Preview

Along with your Recap, the Preview is the simplest speech element to create.

The Preview comes just *before* your Supporting Points, and tells your audience how many Supporting Points there'll be, and what topics they're going to cover.

You might think this would take the "surprise" out of the middle section of your speech. But knowing what's to come actually helps your audience follow you; so it's usually better to tip them off in advance.

The Preview also lets your audience know that you've thought about the structure of your speech, and that you're going to take them someplace worthwhile through a series of orderly and connected steps.

Here's an example of what a Preview sounds like:

> "In the next few minutes, I'm going to share everything you need to know about the Speak Like Yourself approach to public speaking.
>
> "First, we'll look at how to prepare a speech that's valuable to your audience—one that also makes the case for what you want them to do, or do differently.
>
> "Then, I'm going to tell you how to practice. Most people don't practice because they don't know how; but you won't have that problem in the future.
>
> "Finally, we'll look at how you can connect with your audience and deliver your speech with pride. Connecting will help you relax, and will help your audience get the full benefit of your thinking.
>
> (Pause)
>
> "So let's jump right into the first topic: How to prepare a speech that has value and interest for both you and your audience."

See how that works?

If your speech is longer than 10 minutes, do a little mini-recap after each topic, and then a mini-preview of the next. To pick up the example above, you would finish your first Supporting Point (how to prepare a speech) with something like this:

> "So those are the things that are most important when you're putting a speech together.
>
> (Pause)
>
> "Now, let's go on to the second point, which is: How do you practice?"

You do the same thing at the end of your second Supporting Point, and then, when you reach the end of your third Supporting Point, it's time for the Recap.

> Recap

Your Recap is exactly what it sounds like: You remind people of what they've just heard. Don't repeat every little detail—just make this a quick reminder of what's been covered so far. If you've ever hiked a mountain, this is like the pause you take when you've *almost* at the top to look back and see how far you've come. (It also lets you catch your breath before that final push to the summit.)

For the Speak Like Yourself content, above, a Recap might be:

> "So. (pause)
>
> "We've covered a lot of ground in just half an hour.
>
> "First, we talked about the best way to prepare a speech that meets *your audience's* needs, and showcases *your* best thinking.
>
> "Then we looked at some tips for how to practice. Practice makes perfect—but only if you do it right, and you've learned how to practice effectively.
>
> "Finally, we talked about presenting your speech with power, purpose, and pride.
>
> "I hope, by now, you'll agree with me that..."

And you roll right into the second iteration of your Key Message!

> **"So"??**
>
> This Recap example begins with the word "so." It could easily have been "now," or "OK," or another null syllable.
>
> Short words like these let your audience know that you're about to switch gears and they should re-focus their attention. (The pause gives them time to do this.)
>
> They also make your speech more conversational, since this is how people actually talk. In this masterfully folksy speech to the 2012 Democratic National Convention, former President Bill Clinton started 32 out of the 65 paragraphs in his speech with null words, usually "now."

› Your Close

The easiest thing in the world is to lose steam at the end of your speech. You've been working hard, concentrating like a banshee, and maybe fighting off some nervous tension while delivering a great presentation.

Now the finish line is in sight and you start... deflating... like a runner who... just... can't... pull that... final... spurt... of...

Don't do this!

Your speech isn't over until you leave the stage. Pull it together, focus your energy, get ready for that last sprint, deliver a strong Key Message, and then Close by asking for something.

What you ask for can be specific or general, concrete or abstract, but it must "pay off" (complete the promise of) your Key Message.

- If your speech is about *career options for older adults*, don't close by mentioning that there are good career options for young people, too. Tell your audience how to get more information, and wish them good luck in their late-in-life careers.
- If your speech is about *the power of local investing*, don't close by asking people to buy mutual funds. Ask them to invest locally, or lobby for changes in the tax laws that would make this easier to do.

- If I'm talking about the three *Speak Like Yourself* steps to great public speaking, it wouldn't make sense to "close" by asking people to speak more clearly or use bigger words. Instead, I should ask them to try out the three *Speak Like Yourself* steps, and to call me for speaker coaching if they need help!

> Putting It All Together

OK, you've learned about each of the elements that goes into a full-length presentation. From left to right, they are:

1. Your Attention Grabber
2. Your Key Message
3. A Preview of Your Supporting Points
4. Your Supporting Points (which may have Supporting Points of their own)
5. A Recap of Your Supporting Points
6. Your Key Message, and
7. Your Close (complete with what you're asking for)

Let's look at how they work together to turn the Instant Speech about **Speak Like Yourself Steps** into a presentation that could be 10 minutes, 30 minutes, or an hour long.

Instant Speech Example:
Can Anyone Become a Great Public Speaker?

KM: **Yes!** *Anyone* **can develop their public speaking strengths and skills by following these three Speak Like Yourself steps:**
SP: First, prepare a speech that's valuable to your audience.
SP: Then, practice delivering it powerfully. And finally,
SP: Connect with your listeners, and present your speech with pride!
KM: **By following these three simple Speak Like Yourself steps,** *anyone* **can develop their public speaking strengths and skills— and become a good, or even a** *great,* **public speaker!**

To scale up to a full presentation, add the next speech elements.

Can Anyone Become a Great Public Speaker?

Attention Grabber: About one person in eight has the kind of fear of public speaking that gets you a medical diagnosis. (Pause) The rest of us are just plain scared. But that fear tends to diminish when you realize that...

Key Message: *...by following the three Speak Like Yourself steps,* <u>anyone</u> *can develop their public speaking strengths and skills—and become a good, or even* <u>great</u>, *public speaker.*

Preview: In the next few minutes, I'm going to share everything you need to know about the Speak Like Yourself approach to public speaking.

First, we'll look at how to *prepare* a speech that's valuable to your audience—one that also makes the case for what you want them to do, or do differently.

Then, I'm going to tell you how to *practice*. Most people don't practice because they don't know how; but you won't have that problem in the future.

Finally, we'll look at how you can *connect* with your audience and deliver your speech with pride. Connecting will help you relax, and will help your audience get the full benefit of your thinking.

(Pause)

So let's jump right into the first topic: How to prepare a speech that has value and interest for both you *and* your audience.

Supporting Points: [NOTE: Here's where you'll discuss the three Supporting Points you just previewed. The length of those discussions is going to vary according to the length of your speech.

[You could spend three minutes, thirty minutes, or three hours on each Supporting Point. (Or if you really get inspired, you can go on for the length of an entire book!) But generally, each Supporting Point will take about a third of your planned speaking time, after you've deducted 5-10 minutes for the other elements.]

Recap: So. (pause)

We've covered a lot of ground in just a half an hour.

First, we talked about the best way to prepare a speech that meets *your audience's* needs, and showcases *your* best thinking.

Then we looked at some tips for how to practice. Practice makes perfect—but only if you do it right.

And finally, we talked about presenting your speech with power, purpose, and pride.

I hope, by now, you'll agree with me that...

Key Message: *...anyone can develop their public speaking strengths and skills by following the three Speak Like Yourself steps. Which means that anyone can become a good, or even a great, public speaker!*

Close: So.

Here's what I want you to do:

The next time you get a chance to speak in public, don't go and hide somewhere! Say yes, and use this opportunity to put the **Speak Like Yourself** method to work.

I hope that you'll *have fun* using these three easy steps... and *following your strengths and skills to great public speaking.*

And if you need any help, I hope that you'll call me.

Isn't that neat?

Of course it takes practice to turn five sentences into a full-length presentation; but I hope you can see that it's not really *hard*.

Your Key Message requires lots of thought. The choice of Supporting Points may involve some research or reflection. Your Attention Grabber might take time. But once you have those elements in place, filling in the other elements can be as simple as "painting by the numbers."

And, best of all, the energy you save by following this proven and straightforward approach can be applied to other speechmaking skills like practicing (Chapters 8 and 9) and connecting with your audience (Chapter 10).

Okay.

You now know how to *prepare* a speech!

But before we go on to discuss PowerPoint, and the other two **Speak Like Yourself Steps**, there are three questions people often ask at this point:

> "Do I Have to Write Out My Entire Speech?"

The answer is almost always *no*.

There are, occasionally, situations that are so fraught or so delicate that you need to be in control of every single word you say. In that case, you should write out your entire speech, word-for-word, and then *stick to your script.*

But realistically, how often does that happen? Unless you're a high-level diplomat, a spokesperson, or involved in a major legal battle, it's hard to imagine why you would need to be *that* precise about what you're saying.

Instead, for most public speaking scenarios, I recommend a combination of scripting and bullet points.

Use Scripting When You Need to Be Focused and Precise

Scripting (writing something out word-for-word) is the way to approach any section of your speech that needs to be exact.

Maybe you need to give a complex explanation, and want to be sure that you're being clear. In that case, write out your words, test them on someone who doesn't already know what you're explaining, and get their feedback. Then practice delivering those words as *written*; because they'll probably be clearer than anything you could ad lib.

Other things you might want to script out include:

- An historic reference, or anything factual that you could easily get wrong
- A thank you, introduction, or acknowledgment that covers many people (don't trust your memory on this; you're likely to leave someone out!)
- Any transitions that aren't intuitive. Script out exactly how you're going to walk your audience from Point A to Point B if you think you'll have trouble remembering just what connects dish soap to the demographics of India
- Your opening and close (including, importantly, what you're going to ask for!)

Use Bullet Points for Things You Know Well

Have you ever gotten one of those telemarketing calls where, no matter what you do, the person won't go off script? (Of course you have!)

That kind of mechanical stiffness is just what you *don't* want in a speech.

So whenever you're talking about *something you know*, just use a few bullet points or words to remind yourself of the points you want to cover, and any specific facts or statements you want to remember to include.

Then speak to your audience in the same conversational tone you'd use with a few close friends. After all, this is a topic that you *know*.

Scripting is a Moving Target

Your "speaking script" (the one you'll use to practice with, and perhaps take on stage when you're giving your talk) may change as you keep working on a speech.

Some things that you wrote out word-for-word in the beginning will become second nature, as you practice; you can change them into bullet points.

And conversely, you may find that some things you thought you could discuss using bullet points would benefit from being written out.

Keep your speaking script up to date; and when you finally get up to give your speech, you'll have a document that gives you only the prompts you need.

You won't be looking at too many words, or too few.

Instead, what you'll have will be just right.

> "Do I Need to Memorize My Script?"

Again, the answer is almost always *no*.

The problem with memorizing is that it's based on *knowing every single word*. You build a house of cards in your mind, and if you forget one word or phrase, or if something in the room distracts you, your confidence or concentration can break and the whole thing can come tumbling down.

Instead, go for what's called *internalization*. Internalization is a state of familiarity with your speech that lets you pretty much know what's coming next without remembering it word-for-word.

Internalizing your speech will give you a *flexible* sense of security, without trapping you in a fixed set of words. It's a stronger, and more satisfying, approach to public speaking—and one that you'll learn how to achieve in Chapter 8.

> "Should *Every* Speech Be an Instant Speech?"

While the Instant Speech approach works for many, or most, public speaking situations, there *are* some types of speeches that are best developed with a different method. These include:

The Memoir / Biographical / Personal Experience Speech

The goal here is to tell what happened, in chronological order.

Sometimes your story will fall into the equivalent of three Supporting Points (Beginning, Middle, and End); but if it doesn't, don't worry: Just talk about what happened in the order you lived or experienced it.

Do, however, come up with a Key Message, whether or not you end up including it in your speech. Typical Key Message for personal stories are, "This experience taught me that I can survive anything," or "I hope you won't make the same mistakes that I did." Even if you don't say those words when you present, identifying the core point of your speech will help you organize your thoughts, choose which details to leave in or take out, and place every event that you describe in a larger context.

The Research or Progress Report

If you work for a consulting firm, or are presenting scientific data for review, you may be forced to follow industry standards for how to prepare and present your work. Try, however, to add a Key Message, and perhaps even divide your findings into three topic areas or stages of work.

As with any public speech, the structure that you create will help your audience remember what they hear, and will point them toward your desired conclusion. (Think about the difference between a report that begins with the comment, "Here are the results from our study so far," versus one that begins, "We're very excited about what our study has revealed so far.")

If you don't supply a big, true, and important Key Message for your audience, they will supply their own—and it may not be the one you want.

The Workshop or Training Presentation

Rarely does a body of knowledge fall into the simplified parameters of a speech. Instead, most workshops or training sessions are organized around the information they present, and follow an experiential format, such as:

- Explanation–exercise–explanation–exercise; or
- Explanation–discussion–exercise–explanation–discussion–exercise.

It can be useful, however, to structure your explanations as Instant Speeches or full-length presentations. This will help *you* keep your participants engaged, and will help *them* understand and remember your explanations.

Take-Away

It isn't hard to grow an Instant Speech into a full-length presentation. Most of the expanded length will come from new material added to your Supporting Points (and if your Supporting Points become long or complicated, turn them into mini-Instant Speeches, for better comprehension). But you'll also need to add an Attention Grabber, Preview, Recap, and Close to create a fully rounded experience for your audience.

Take a flexible approach to how much of your speech you'll write out versus delivering from bullet points. Only script out the places where you'll need to use exact wording; and be aware that what you need to be prompted on may change as you practice your speech.

Finally, don't forget that, while an Instant Speech is your best starting point in most public speaking situations, there are exceptions to that rule.

> Chapter 7

Don't Be Afraid of PowerPoint

In Chapter 6, you learned how to create the *verbal* part of a full-length presentation.

But in today's public speaking environment, most audiences will expect your words to be accompanied by some kind of visual, usually PowerPoint.

I happen to think that's a good thing.

PowerPoint—or Keynote, its more intuitive Apple equivalent—can be a great tool for holding your audience's attention. And it can also help you develop and refine your speech.

> But Didn't You Say PowerPoint Would Doom Us to Fail?

Not quite.

You probably remember that the three **Doomed to Fail** steps are:

Doomed to Fail Step 1: Find Out Everything You Can about Your Topic
Doomed to Fail Step 2: Put Your Facts into PowerPoint
Doomed to Fail Step 3: Ignore Your Speech Until the Day You Give It

You might think, from the starring role that *PowerPoint* plays in this formula, that *PowerPoint* is making us bad speakers.

But you can't blame PowerPoint for what we've done to ourselves since PowerPoint was introduced in 1990.

As Cassius said in Act 1, Scene 2 of Shakespeare's **Julius Caesar**, "The fault, dear Brutus, is not in our stars, But in ourselves, that we are underlings."

We have made ourselves the servants, the underlings, of PowerPoint by:

- Using it as a dumping ground for ill-considered data; and

- Filling it with words that make us superfluous.

And the sad thing is, it would be just as easy—easier—to let PowerPoint *enhance* our presentations, instead of using it in a way that confuses, annoys, and bores our audiences.

> Just Whose Speech Is This, Anyway?

In Chapter 5, I showed you how the **Speak Like Yourself Steps** to great public speaking could be turned into an Instant Speech. If you typed the five sentences of that speech into a single Keynote or PowerPoint slide, it would look like this:

Can *Anyone* Become a Great Public Speaker?

- Yes, anyone can develop their public speaking strengths and skills by following these three **Speak Like Yourself** steps:

  - First, prepare a speech that's valuable to your audience.

  - Then, practice delivering it powerfully. And finally,

  - Connect with your listeners, and present your speech with pride!

- By following these three **Speak Like Yourself** steps, *anyone* can develop their public speaking strengths and skills—and become a good, or even <u>great</u>, public speaker!

This slide, in my humble opinion, has way too many words.

But worse, those words stand alone. Anyone who reads the slide can understand it fully. They don't need a *speaker* to explain it to them.

If you're the person delivering this speech, think about the conflict this creates for both you and your audience:

- The slide says everything *you* want to say, so the only remaining jobs for you are to either read it, summarize it, or embellish it. None of these are powerful roles. In essence, *you* are supporting the slide, rather than *it* supporting you.

- Because reading is faster than speaking, your audience will finish reading the slide before you have finished talking about it. Now they have to decide whether to listen to you repeat what they've already read, or tune out until you catch up with them—at which point they may, or may not, tune back into what you're saying.

This is not a good situation: You never want to delegate your role as *the presenter* to a slide! And you don't want to fight a slide for your audience's attention; that's always a losing battle.

Fortunately, there's a solution to this problem. It involves *listening* to PowerPoint as you create your slides!

> Your Slide Is Trying to Tell You Something

As I was putting together the example slide to the left, there was a moment when it looked like this:

> # Can *Anyone* Become a Great Public Speaker?
>
> - Yes, anyone can develop their public speaking strengths and skills by following these three **Speak Like Yourself** steps:
>   - First, prepare a speech that's valuable to your audience.
>   - Then, practice delivering it powerfully. And finally,

At this point, the slide was *full*. When I kept typing, the size of my text (font size) *shrunk* to accommodate the new words. (Compare this slide to the previous one to see how much smaller the text got.)

Believe it or not, reducing your font size is PowerPoint or Keynote's way of telling you to *stop typing* because you're overcrowding your slide.

- When this happens, there are three things you can do:
- Ignore the message that PowerPoint is trying to give you, and keep typing (that's what people usually do);
- Edit down what you've already written so there's room for more words on your slide; or
- Split your discussion into two or more slides, so that each slide holds just a single idea.

In general, the third choice is your best.

That's because putting *just one idea* on each slide allows you to talk about just one thing for as much or as little time as you want, without your audience jumping ahead to the new point that's lower down on your slide.

(The usual solution of building a slide up line by line rarely makes sense. If each line stands alone anyway, why not give each line its own slide, instead of crowding them all together?)

But what if you want to present an *overview* of your content? In that case, editing it down so that everything fits on one slide can be a good solution; like this:

How to Become a Great Public Speaker

- Develop your strengths and skills
- Prepare a valuable speech
- Practice delivering it powerfully
- Present with pride
- *You can do it!*

Editing your content has the added benefit of forcing you to identify *the core* of each idea, and then state it as simply as possible.

The slide to the left does that effectively. But it would be stronger if it had a picture.

› Yes, They *Are* Worth 1000 Words

Seth Godin, an internet marketer, famously wrote an anti-PowerPoint essay that featured a picture of dead birds.

He said, "Talking about pollution in Houston? Instead of giving me four bullet points of EPA data, why not read me the stats but show me a photo of a bunch of dead birds, some smog and even a diseased lung?"[7]

Godin was right. Slides that have only pictures—or a picture and a title—are more compelling than slides with only bullet points:

But delivering slides that have only images (even when they also have a title) can be a burden for business presenters.

That's because—unlike motivational speakers, who give the exact same speech over and over and over again—business speakers are generally delivering new content each time they present. To make things worse, their content is often developed by others, and they have very little time to study it.

7 http://sethgodin.typepad.com/seths_blog/2007/01/really_bad_powe.html

Given these constraints, it's more than fair for business speakers to create slides that give you more explicit direction. So I recommend this compromise: summary bullets, and one cool picture:

How to Become a Great Public Speaker

- Develop your strengths and skills
- Prepare a valuable speech
- Practice delivering it powerfully
- Present with pride
- *You can do it!*

What I like about this solution is that it:

- Gives *you* (the speaker) enough detail to present this slide without using notes;
- Gives *your audience* the information they need to follow you without getting bogged down; and
- Has both visual and logical appeal.

But the beauty of this slide also lies in what it *doesn't* do. It doesn't:

- Usurp your role as the presenter;
- Overwhelm your audience with words, or multiple pictures or charts; and best of all, doesn't
- Force them to chose between reading and listening—with the result that they end up being dissatisfied with both.

So just to review: If you were listening to a great public speaker communicate on a topic of interest, would you rather be looking at the compromise slide above, or at this one that we started with?

And since you are, or will be, a great public speaker who'll be communicating on a topic of interest—would you rather have your audience read this slide, or listen to you delivering these words?

Can *Anyone* Become a Great Public Speaker?

- Yes, anyone can develop their public speaking strengths and skills by following these three **Speak Like Yourself** steps:

  - First, prepare a speech that's valuable to your audience.

  - Then, practice delivering it powerfully. And finally,

  - Connect with your listeners, and present your speech with pride!

- By following these three **Speak Like Yourself** steps, *anyone* can develop their public speaking strengths and skills—and become a good, or even *great*, public speaker!

> Great Slides, Like Great Speeches, Are a Process

Everything about great speechmaking is a moving target, and your slides are no exception:

- The first time you tell a story, it may have too many details;
- The first time you talk through a speech, you'll probably present too many ideas; and
- The first time you create slides, they'll probably be too dense and wordy.

So keep in mind that there's nothing wrong with creating text-heavy slides on your first try.

The trick is to *not stop at your first try*. Don't settle for slapping ideas into PowerPoint and walking away, as most people do. Instead:

- Save your wordy first-draft version to use as a handout or leave-behind for your audience.
- Then copy the words from those first draft slides into a Word (or Pages) document, or into PowerPoint's Notes feature. They can become the basis for your speaking script—the words that will prompt you when you give the speech.
- Now create a second, more streamlined version of your slides to put onscreen while you're presenting. Make this version as clean and focused as you can. Remember, its purpose is to add *visual interest* to your presentation, and help your audience follow your thinking—not to deliver the presentation for you!

› One More PowerPoint Secret: Slide Sorter

OK, it's not really a secret, but this may be a new perspective for you:

PowerPoint has a feature in its "View" menu called **Slide Sorter**. (Keynote calls it Light Table.) When you click on this option, your slides are displayed as thumbnail images.

Because these thumbnail slides are small, you can view *your entire set of slides* at one time!

There are three ways to use this feature as you prepare and practice your presentation:

Use Slide Sorter to Outline Your Speech

It can be hard to keep the structure of your speech in mind while you're writing out a detailed script. That's why I like to block out speeches in PowerPoint before I begin to actually write them.

To follow this method, start by creating "Placeholder Slides" like these:

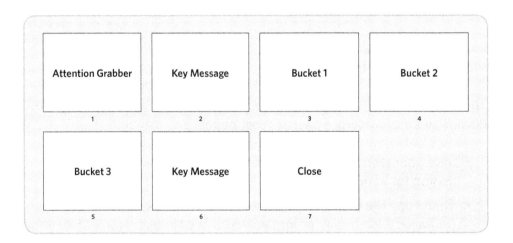

Then, as you begin to develop your thoughts, go back and replace each of those placeholders with slides that hold your actual content. Notice that **you don't have to replace the placeholder slides in any particular order.** Do it as elements become clear to you.

- Whenever you know what your Attention Grabber will be, you can replace the "Attention Grabber" placeholder slide with the slide that will support your actual Grabber. You might choose to show a picture (if your Grabber is a story), a large number (if it's a statistic), a question mark (for a riddle), or a few words that will grab your audience's attention.

- Once you've decided on your Key Message replace the "Key Message" placeholder slides with slides that contain, or support—yes, you guessed it!—your Key Message.

- When you know what your closing Ask will be, replace the placeholder "Close" slide with a statement, question, or phrase that asks for what you want.

- Replace the words "Bucket 1," "Bucket 2," and "Bucket 3" with the titles for each of your Supporting Points. Then follow each of those titles with as many new slides as you need to support, illustrate, or emphasize what you're going to say. (My suggestion is to put a single idea or sub-topic on each slide, so that you see how many ideas are in each bucket, and how well the sections balance each other.)

Use Slide Sorter to Troubleshoot Your Speech

While you're using Slide Sorter to create your speech, you can also use it to get a higher-level view of how well your speech is working.

As you scan your speech in Slide Sorter, ask yourself questions like these:

- Does my Key Message truly set the tone for what follows?

- Does every slide have the same *look and feel*? (Consistency in the appearance of your slides makes it easier for your audience to decode what they say.)

- Do any of them have too many words, or too much data? (If so, which words, phrases or ideas can you take out? (Remember that you can take things out of your slides without taking them out of your speech!)

- Do the charts or graphs *reinforce* my point, or obscure it?

- Are the three buckets about equally full? (If one Supporting Point has 18 slides and the other two have three slides each, you have a balance problem.)

- Does every section lead into the next? (If not, your buckets might be out of order, or might not be *like each other,* as described in Chapter 6.)
- Do I build to a powerful Close, and ask the audience for what I want?

These, and other, similar questions, are much easier to answer if you're looking at Slide Sorter View than if you're scanning a 30-page script and trying to hold page 5 in your mind so that you can compare it to page 27.

Use Slide Sorter to Help You *Learn* Your Speech

You may be surprised to hear that *learning* and *practicing* a speech are actually the same activity. In Chapter 8, I'll show you how to learn and practice your speech with PowerPoint, and how to use Slide Sorter to make that process easier.

But first, there's one more PowerPoint-related issue that we should address:

> And Finally: Don't Use PowerPoint to Hide

One reason for the enduring popularity of Bad PowerPoint is that it can be used to hide two things: Yourself, and your ideas.

This actual slide, used by the U.S. Army, caused an Internet sensation when it was revealed in the **New York Times**.[8]

The **Times** reported that, on being shown this slide, General Stanley A. McChrystal, the leader of American and NATO forces in Afghanistan, "dryly remarked, 'When we understand that slide, we'll have won the war.'"

The joke, of course, is that this slide will never reveal how to win the war. In fact, it probably can't reveal *anything* comprehensible—and perhaps that was the point. (And lest you think that only the government would create this level of obfuscation, recall the last business presentation you heard. You probably saw many slides with a comparable lack of clarity.)

That's how people use PowerPoint to hide the point they're "trying" to make.

[8] "We Have Met the Enemy and He Is PowerPoint," by Elisabeth Bumiller, April 26, 2012, http://www.nytimes.com/2010/04/27/world/27PowerPoint.html

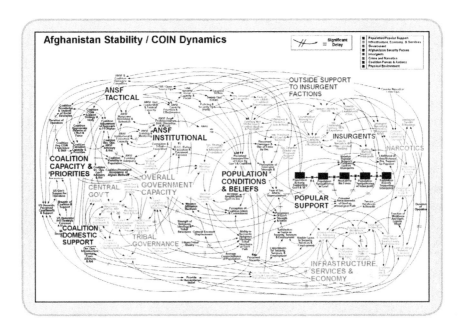

But the other, and perhaps more important, thing that it's easy to hide with Bad PowerPoint is *yourself*. Here's how that works:

- If your audience is spending most of its energy decoding and detangling what's on the screen, they're not going to pay much attention to you;

- If your PowerPoint indicates a sloppy frame of mind or a lack of logical discipline, your audience will lower its expectations of you and—presto!—you're off the hook; and

- If you're unfamiliar with your PowerPoint, most of your energy will go into nervously looking over your shoulder to see which slide you're on, reacting with surprise and dismay when you click to the next slide and don't recognize it, fumbling around for the point each slide is trying to make, and reading endless lists of bullets that you then embellish with ill-conceived asides.

The net effect is that your audience will dismiss or ignore you, and you won't really notice them.

Aren't you glad that isn't *your* game plan?

So, now that you know how to prepare a speech—and a PowerPoint— that's valuable to your audience, let's look at how practicing can help you bring it powerfully to the stage.

Take-Away

While lots of people love to hate PowerPoint, it can be a flexible and useful tool at many stages of the speechmaking process: It's a good outlining tool; it can give you an overview of your speech; and, as you'll see in the next chapter, it can help you learn your speech.

The key is to use each slide to support just one of your ideas in a way that helps hold your audience's interest. Don't put your speaking notes in your slides, because doing so means that you've given up your role as the presenter. And if your slides depict data, be sure they do it in a way that illuminates rather than obfuscating your point.

If you keep those tips in mind, and put some thought into creating it, PowerPoint and Keynote can enhance your public speaking instead of detracting from it.

> Chapter 8

Practice Makes Perfect... But Only If You Practice Right

You've prepared a wonderful speech, and a PowerPoint that makes it even more interesting.

Now it's time to bridge the gap between *preparing* your speech, and presenting it.

That bridging activity is called *practice.* And while *practicing* may look about as appealing as jumping off the proverbial cliff there really *is* a path you can take to smoothly and safely reach the other side.

> Yeah, But I *Hate* Practicing

Welcome to the club.

Many people hate to practice. If they even get *near* the activity, it leaves them feeling bruised, beat up, and hopeless about the possibility of ever getting better at public speaking (or anything else).

Not by coincidence, those of us who hate to practice are the same "those of us" who hate making "mistakes"—because making mistakes is what practicing is all about.

The Catch-22 of Practicing

Ironically, the more we don't practice because we're afraid of hearing ourselves sound less than perfect... the more less than perfect we sound.

Remember that, in most cases, we're practicing something that *we don't yet know how to do.* If we already knew how to do it, we'd be *polishing*, or *perfecting*, or *maintaining*, or *reinforcing* our skills.

But by definition, if we're *practicing*, we're working on a skill we haven't acquired yet. And boy, can acquiring a new skill be tough on the old ego!

For people who are perfectionists, or highly self-critical, or inclined to pessimism, practicing can be a particular hell. To find out if you're in that group, see if you agree with any of these statements:

- "I cringe every time I make a mistake."
- "I *should* be able to do this better."
- "I hate knowing that my performance is disappointing to others."
- "This is so discouraging; I'll probably never do it well."

If you're old friends with any of these feelings, you probably suffer when you practice.

Worse, you'll probably struggle even harder to learn a new skill than you otherwise might. That's because it's easier to learn when we're open, excited, and eager to push our imperfect selves up the growth curve that it is when we're closed-down, self-protective, and paranoid about being inadequate.

So starting right now, I'd like you to *choose an attitude* toward the process of acquiring public speaking skills. (Choosing an attitude is basically play-acting. You pick the role you want to play, and then "fake it 'till you make it.")

Your choices are:

Attitude A: "I'm not a great public speaker yet, so I must be a complete and utter failure."

Attitude B: "I'm not a great public speaker yet, but I plan to become one."

You can probably guess which attitude I recommend!

> Why Practice? To Become Unconscious!

Whenever we acquire a new skill, we go through four predictable stages:

1. Unconscious Incompetence

Ignorance is bliss at this stage of the process, when you literally don't know that there's something you don't know.

2. Conscious Incompetence

In this phase, you've somehow become aware of the skill that you're lacking. You set out to acquire it, taking awkward baby steps at first.

3. Conscious Competence

You've been working hard on your new skill and if you *really concentrate*, you can actually put what you've learned to use—at least some of the time!

If you're a glass-half-full kind of person, you'll be thrilled to watch yourself making steady progress toward your goal. If you're a glass-half-empty type, you may be discouraged or even depressed at how long it takes to move through this phase, or at how imperfectly you still do this new thing.

And then, one morning, you wake up and find that you've finally achieved...

4. Unconscious Competence

You can now reliably use your new skill without having to monitor your every move.

For some people, this is paradise. For others, it's a brief pit stop before they start thinking about how cool it would be to get even better.

So, yes, we practice in order to become unconscious—or rather, unconsciously competent.

Of course, the catch is that **the time when practicing is most important is during stages two and three** of the learning process. Precisely the time when, unless you're a very self-confident person, you may already be feeling awkward, inept, or vulnerable.

So take a tip from Attitude B, above, and remind yourself often that, while you're not a great public speaker *yet*, you're in the process of becoming one.

The Myth That Only Junior People Practice

When I was writing corporate speeches, it was understood that the higher an executive's rank, the less likely he (yes, he was usually a "he") was to practice in front of other people.

Of course, the *best* high-ranking leaders—the ones who truly care about motivating and persuading their "troops"—practice often and conscientiously. But since these top people tend to practice in private with just a coach and a trusted colleague or two present, the unfortunate myth that they're "natural" communicators, and that only junior people need to practice, persists.

> OK, I'm Ready. Now What Do I Do?

Practicing is, at bottom, pretty simple:

With all due respect to coaches and trainers like myself, who'll walk you through a more specific and individually focused process, the basic activity is nothing more than trial-and-error with a little personal taste thrown in.

Here's what you do:

1. **Read** a *small* section of your speech out loud (or, more formally, "deliver" it using slides as well as notes).
2. **Ask yourself:** "Do I like how that sounded?"
3. **If you like how it sounded,** read or deliver the same thing again, trying to get more comfortable with it.

4. **If you *didn't* like how it sounded**, read or deliver the same thing again, but do it in a slightly different way. (Faster. Slower. With more energy. With more intimacy. Take out some words if it's too wordy. Add some words if it needs more explanation. Etc.)

5. **Repeat steps 2-4.**

That's all there is to it. You read something, tweak it, and read it again, gently pushing the speech (and yourself) toward being smoother, more clear, and more relaxed.

You Know How to Do This

Practice, according to the Random House Unabridged Dictionary of the English Language, is "repeated performance or systematic exercise for the purpose of acquiring skill or proficiency."

We've all practiced *something*—from tying a knot or writing the alphabet to playing a video game or driving a car—but we don't all feel proficient at practicing.

That's OK, though. You'll be proficient soon!

One word of warning, though: As you tweak small portions of your speech, *do not throw the baby out with the bathwater!*

You're more likely to improve your speech by making small changes and observing their effect than by starting from scratch every time you hit a snag.

> How to Practice

Before we get to the all-important topic of **what to practice**, let's look at *how* you can make the process work even more effectively.

To get the full benefit of practicing, do it:

- Out loud
- In character (remember your Avatar?)
- Slowly
- Conversationally
- Often!

You won't be able to achieve *all of these goals* each time you practice. But if you keep them in mind, and strive to do your best, they'll speed your journey to great public speaking.

Here's how (and why) to do each of those things:

Practice Out Loud

As its name implies, public speaking is a *spoken* art form. Which means that you can't practice public speaking without *saying something out loud.*

To put that differently, **editing is not practicing.**

You can write something brilliantly, and edit it a hundred times, but you aren't actually *practicing a speech* until you put down the paper, stand up (perhaps in front of a mirror), and listen to yourself say the words out loud.

Drop that Editing Pen

Even the best speakers can over-edit and under-practice. One of my most skilled clients fell into this mistake when she found herself still "fixing" her speech an hour before she was due to present it.

Though her words were honed to a razor's edge, she didn't deliver them with her usual verve. Her focus and her rhythm were subtly off, and she got thrown by a distraction (dry mouth) that she would normally have been able to shrug off. Her speech was still highly effective, but she knew it wasn't near her best— and being your best is much more fun.

Practice in Character (Remember Your Avatar?)

Whenever you practice *anything* related to communications or public speaking, do your best to *be in your Avatar.*

This means trying to feel relaxed, powerful, confident, authoritative, or whatever else your Avatar feels.

Remember that your Avatar needs constant reinforcement. It isn't something you can snap into on command for 20 minutes once a year. Whether your Avatar is Corporate Girl, Salsa Steve, Brilliant Barbara, or Fearless Francisco, your ability to become him or her on Speech Day will depend on how much time the two of you spend together in advance.

Practice Slowly

This is a fast-paced world, and very few of us get told that we should *talk faster.*

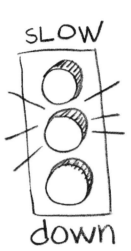

Of course, when you're practicing a public communication, the need to slow down is even greater, for one very simple reason: *If you speak too quickly, no one will hear (or remember) what you're saying.*

I like to think of this in terms of the speed of light and sound:

- **Light travels *fast***, at about 186,000 miles per second. And we're also used to seeing things quickly and comprehensively. When we look at something, our eyes can absorb the whole image "in a flash," i.e., all at once.
- Compared to light, **sound travels *glacially***, at a mere 340 miles per second. When someone is speaking, we can't grab their meaning in a flash, as we can with a picture. We have to wait for each phrase to unfold in order; and if the speaker rushes past an important point, there's no way for us to go back and recapture it.

Another good reason to practice speaking slowly is that, when you take the stage to give a speech, your heart will speed up.

Your nerves will fire.

And like a racehorse at the gate, you'll start dashing through your presentation—*unless* you've prepared yourself to counter this effect by practicing very *slowly*.

What's the Best Way to Practice Speaking Slowly?

It's *not* to talk in slow motion. This doesn't work, and will make you feel silly.

Instead, practice **pausing at the end of sentences**—and even more importantly, at the **end of each idea**. By doing this, you help your audience catch up, and absorb whatever you just said. (It also helps to *ar-ti-cu-late clear-ly*.)

Practice Conversationally

This is the most important practice tip I can give you:

Whenever you're working on any aspect of a speech, speak conversationally, as if you were talking to a good friend over coffee. (With apologies to the great local coffee shops that deserve your business, I sometimes call this "The Starbucks Strategy.")

The rule is: Don't "speechify," just *talk*.

Does this mean that you can rush, mumble, and pay no attention to how you sound?

No! For people to hear what you're saying, your words must be clear and audible. But you *don't* have to sound as if you just graduated from elocution school.

So if you catch yourself sounding that way when you practice, stop practicing.

Relax, regroup, and come back and try again later.

Practice Often

Instead of carving out a little time to practice every day, most people wait until they have an hour or more available. This means that days or weeks often go by between practice sessions.

That's backwards.

Even if you're incredibly focused and efficient, you're not going to master new presentation skills, or even nail the delivery of a particular speech, by just practicing every so often.

As any athlete or musician can tell you, physical skills—and public speaking is a physical as well as a mental skill—need *short and frequent practice sessions,* for the following very good reasons:

- Daily repetition helps you internalize whatever you're practicing (get it *into* your brain and body), and build muscle memory so that you move more quickly from conscious to unconscious competence.
- If you practice every day, you'll actually *remember* what you did the day before. You can pick up where you left off without having to reinvent the wheel.
- Daily practice keeps you from getting discouraged. You'll see yourself making slow, steady progress, and you'll feel good about the quality of your commitment; and finally,
- When you practice every day—all right, *most* days—you never have to waste time wondering if today is a day that you're going to practice. The answer to that question is always *yes!*

So, 'nuff said? Practice a little bit each day!

> How to Practice Your Speech

Finally—the **what to do** portion of our program!

Before I tell you what to do, though, there is a caveat: I'm not going to suggest a "typical" practice session (there is no such thing), or tell you what to do every day because, when you're working on a speech, every practice session will be unique.

That's because every practice session builds on the ones that came before it.

As your skills build, your focus will change. The things you worked on last week won't be your primary concern this week, because they'll already be in much better shape.

You'll also want to *make changes* to your practice routine.

Public speaking is a *dynamic* activity that takes place in a live environment where many factors (including your mood) can shift. So practicing in a static way—the same thing, over and over, each day—isn't a good way to prepare yourself for the sometimes unexpected demands of speechmaking.

That said, here are the things that I work on, in the general order in which I approach them:

Is Public Speaking Coaching for You?

Part of becoming a better public speaker is learning how to assess what *you* need to work on. And as you practice more, you'll get better at practicing, just as you'll get better at public speaking.

Along the way, though, most people find they can benefit from consulting a qualified public speaking coach. In my other world, music, even the most accomplished players will take occasional lessons or master classes with someone whose skills are more advanced than theirs.

Public speaking is a lot like music or sports, in that you'll be doing most of the work! But just like in those two others fields, an experienced coach can save you time and effort by pointing out things you can profitably work on.

Talk-Through

Before you attempt to deliver, or even read through, your speech, *talk through* what you're going to be doing.

That means talking to yourself, and telling the "story" of your speech, out loud.

"OK, first I'm going to start by talking about the biggest corporate event I ever worked on. Then I'm going to give my key message, which is that if people would focus on saying things that *actually make sense*, a lot of business errors would be caught a lot faster. Then I'm going to preview my three buckets. Then I'm going to talk about..."

As you can see, when you talk through a presentation, you're not actually working on *content*.

Instead, you're drilling *the flow of your presentation,* going section by section through a description of what ideas the speech will cover.

In Chapter 6, I talked about why *internalizing* a speech—imprinting it with your mind and muscle memory—is far superior to *memorizing*, or learning it be rote.

Well, that's what a talk-through it for. It helps you internalize the points in your speech, in order.

After you've done this a few times, and feel like you know what's going on, your next step is to actually practice giving the speech. This is called a...

Stumble-Through

The first time you read through or deliver your presentation out loud is *the only time you'll ever hear it with totally fresh ears.*

So use this opportunity to get a general gut-check as to whether you think it holds together.

As you're reading, or talking with bullet points, ask yourself:

- Do the points I'm making sound convincing?
- Are my arguments laid out well?
- Are certain sections repetitive? Or, conversely, too "thin"?

Take a critical ear to your content—but **don't critique the way you're reading.** In fact, don't worry about your speaking style at all, right now. That's not the point of a stumble-through, which is to let you get re-acquainted with the content of your speech.

If you decide that part of your speech is too long, or too dense, or too short, or too slight, fix it, and then do another stumble-through.

Practice Your Key Message

Once you've finished stumbling, it's time to take your speech apart and start working more intensively on shorter sections. This means focusing on:

- Your speech's most important elements; and
- The areas that need extra work.

Of your main elements, nothing is more important to practice than your Key Message. This is the entire crux of your speech, and you have to know it well enough to deliver it with conviction.

So learn your key message inside out, backwards and forwards, and be able to say it while you're asleep and standing on your head. (I like to tell my clients that I'm going to call them at 3AM and ask them what their key message is; but so far, I haven't done it.)

As you repeat your Key Message, try to keep it sounding fresh. Every time you say it, try to feel as if you're saying it—or better yet, *thinking* it—for the very first time.

Practice Your Attention Grabber

Now that your Key Message is rock solid, practice *leading into it* with your Attention Grabber.

If your Attention Grabber is a story, you'll need to figure out how much detail you need to make your point, without bogging things down? (In Chapter 9, you'll learn more about how to shape and practice stories.)

Try telling your Attention Grabber in different ways. You can record it and listen back, if you'd like, or ask a friend for his or her opinion; but you'll also form an opinion from just listening to yourself as you speak.

Decide which approach seems to work the best, and then ruthlessly *cut out any details or explanations that don't contribute* to the desired effect.

Finally, don't be discouraged if it takes 10 or even 20 tries to shape your story in a way that works. Few of us can tell a story well the first, or even the tenth time we try. But the effort you put in here will be repaid when you're able to capture an audience's interest.

> ### What If My Attention Grabber Isn't a Story?
>
> Even if your Grabber is a question, or a surprising fact, think of it as telling a *story*. Like a story, your question or fact has a *set-up* and a *pay-off*. Like a story, its success is largely dependent on good *timing*. And as with a story, its purpose is to catch your audience's attention. So whatever your Attention Grabber's format, practice delivering it as carefully as you'd practice a story.

Practice the Other Stories in Your Presentation

Now give the other stories in your presentation the same focused attention you gave to your Attention Grabber.

Once you're satisfied with how they sound, try your stories out on someone who hasn't heard them yet. Ask your listener to tell you whether or not they:

- Make sense;
- Hold his or her attention; and
- Support (or illustrate) the points they're supposed to be supporting (or illustrating).

Practice Listing Your Supporting Points

You've now arrived at the fat center of your speech, and its important that you internalize *its* structure by once again drilling what's going to happen.

Use the talk-through technique described above, focusing only on your Supporting Points, as in:

> "The first think I'm going to do is present Supporting Point number one, which is **prepare** a speech that's valuable for your audience.
>
> "Then, Supporting Point number two is about how you should **practice** it powerfully.

"The last Supporting Point is to **connect** with the audience and **present** with pride.

"Prepare, practice, present with pride. Prepare, practice, present with pride..."

"Walking and Talking" When You Practice

If you hear a rhythm in that last paragraph, it's the rhythm of me talking through my points while I walk down the street, or pace around a room. For me, "walking and talking" is a good way to get my body, as well as my brain, into the act.

It also helps circumvent my NLV (that Nasty Little Voice we discussed in Chapter 1), since the combined effort of remembering whatever I'm practicing, saying it out loud, and not bumping into the furniture doesn't leave many brain cells free for self-criticism.

Practice Your Supporting Points Out of Order

Whether you've written out your speech or will use slides, bullet points, or an outline as your speaking script, it's now time to practice *the content of your Supporting Points.*

As with your Key Message or Attention Grabber, don't practice your Supporting Points once and then call it a day.

Keep running through them, out loud, until they're firmly in your comfort zone.

And then, start shaking that comfort zone up.

Part of internalizing a speech means taking it apart and putting it back together again— mixing, matching, and shuffling sections—so that you don't become dependent on always starting from the beginning and going straight through to the end.

The reason for this, as we've noted before, is that public speaking rarely works that way.

More commonly, your mike shorts out. A waiter drops a tray. Something distracts you, and you lose your place.

If you've only practiced in lock step, this real-life experience will be a shock.

So don't always practice Supporting Point 1, then Supporting Point 2, then Supporting Point 3, even if you're going to deliver them in this order (well, of course you are!). Instead, practice your Supporting Points out of order—and shuffle up the content *within* each Supporting Point, too.

That way, if anything throws you off track, you'll always know that you can find your way back.

Practice Everything Else Out of Order, Too!

Now it's time for the big mix-and-match. Make up your own jumbled practice routine, such as:

- Talk through the middle of your speech, then jump to the top (beginning) and pick it up there.
- Tell a story from your second bucket, followed by your Attention Grabber.
- Deliver your Close. Now your Preview. Now your Key Message.

You would think that all this jumping around is confusing; but in fact, it works the opposite way.

The more you practice jumping around your speech, the more thoroughly you'll come to know it—and the more easily it will unfold *in the right order* when you finally deliver it to an audience.

Practice Your Transitions

At the end of all this mixing and matching, put your speech back in order, and practice it from beginning to end again.

But this time, rather than focusing on what's inside each section, work on *getting from one section to the next.*

In other words, practice your "transitions."

Transitions include the Preview and Recap sections that we discussed in Chapter 6, but they can also be *any* short phrase that gets you from what you're talking about now to whatever you're going to talk about next.

As you know from the discussion of Previews and Recaps, transitions don't have to be clever, they just have to be *clear*. So with that in mind, practice moving between speech sections by using little formula phrases like:

> "Now that we'll talked about X, let's take a look at Y."
>
> "So far, we've looked at X and Y. Now let's turn to Z."
>
> "If you find X, Y, and Z persuasive, I hope that you'll..."
>
> "I want to start with a little story about..."
>
> "What I conclude from this is that..."
>
> "In just a minute, we'll get to A. But first, I want to talk about..."

The beauty of these simple comments is that *they keep both you and your audience oriented*, like road signs that signal you're about to take a turn.

And like clear signs along a highway, they make the journey go more smoothly, and reassure everyone that you're on track.

Practice Your Close

The easiest thing in the world is to reach the end of your speech and dribble off.

And, believe it or not, that's even *more* likely to happen if you always practice your speech from the beginning to the end.

That's because, by the time you reach the end of your speech (and the end of your practice session), your energy will be depleted. This means, in turn, that if you always practice from beginning to end, *you're always practicing your close*—arguably the most important moment of your speech, since it's the last thing your audience hears—*when you're already tired.*

Don't do this.

Practice your Close early and often, so that it gets the energy it deserves.

And don't forget to close your Close by asking your audience for what you want!

Practice Whatever Else Needs It

By now, you know your speech quite well; and *you know the places where it's weak.*

Every speech has its own tricky sections, whether they're complicated stories, or difficult transitions, or technical explanations that need to be streamlined.

Those are the places the need the most work; but ironically, they're also the parts that you're most likely to skip over when you practice, because you hate facing them.

OK, you're human, but don't give in to this temptation! Get out your metaphoric flashlight and shine it on the dark and dank places in your speech.

You owe it to yourself and your audience to make **your entire speech** as good as it can be.

Can You Practice Too Much?

Lots of people worry that, if they practice "too much," they'll lose their edge. But in reality, the edge they're talking about is the edge of the cliff that you'll be dangling over if you don't *know your speech* before you give it.

Unless you really love cliffhanging terror (and some people do), you're better off practicing "too much" than too little. You're better off knowing your content inside out than grasping at straws while people watch.

To keep things fresh when you *give* your speech, just focus on your audience. Trust me, being present in the moment will give you all the thrills you need!

> How to Practice with PowerPoint or Keynote

Up until now, I've described the practicing process, as if your slides exist in a parallel universe that's completely separate from the words you'll be saying.

Of course, that's not true. At some point, you'll need to practice your content and your slides together.

But that point doesn't have to be at the very beginning. (It also shouldn't be the very end, as in, five minutes before you give your speech; but you already knew that, right?)

My suggestion is that you start working on your content first. Then, as you become more familiar and more comfortable with your speech, add your slides into the practicing mix.

When you're ready to do that, here's what to work on:

Practice Not Reading Your Slides

As we discussed in Chapter 7, you don't ever want to deliver your *slides*. You want to deliver a *speech*, and have the slides support *you*, rather than the other way around.

So as you practice with PowerPoint or Keynote, be sure that you're not just mindlessly reading what the people in your audience can read for themselves. (If a particular slide is very wordy—sometimes this is out of your control—be sure that you say *less* than what's on the slide, not more.)

The only exception to the rule of not reading from your slides is when you're citing a quote that you want people to both see and hear. Here's a quote, from a speech I often give to women professionals, that I read out loud, word for word, because it's that important. (The quote refers to Andrea Kramer's discovery that, if someone was underselling themselves in her law firm's self-evaluation process, that someone was invariably female.[9])

> ## "I would know *without looking at the name* whether the memo was submitted by a man or a woman."
>
> **Andrea S. Kramer, Esq.**
> **"Bragging Rights: Self-Evaluation Dos and Don'ts"**

[9] ***Bragging Rights: Self-Evaluation Dos and Don'ts,*** by Andrea S. Kramer, Esq., was originally published in the National Association of Women Lawyers Journal, Summer, 2007. A downloadable PDF is posted at http://speakupforsuccess.com/287/bragging-rights

Practice What You'll Say to Transition from One Slide to the Next

In Chapter 7, I talked about using the transitions between slides to create forward motion; and earlier in this chapter, we looked at how to transition between sections of your speech.

Good transitions are one of the single most effective things you can do to keep people with you when you're presenting. So as you practice delivering your speech with slides, be sure to practice your transitions.

Few people address that challenge, which is why, in so many business speeches, you hear presenters saying, "And this slide shows... and this slide shows... and this slide shows... and this slide shows..."

Practice Using a "Clicker"

Part of creating a smooth transition is knowing when to click up your next slide.

If you do a lot of presenting, it's worth investing in a Presentation Remote—discussed later in this chapter under "Useful Tools for Practicing"—so that you can develop your "click" timing.

Incorporate the Remote ("clicker") into your practice, and, as you get more comfortable and confident, start using it to advance your slides in a way that makes each new slide an event. For example:

> "Why do we think this plan will work? The main reason is, because... (click)
>
> (pause)
>
> ...**60%** of your current customers have told us that's what *they* believe."

This kind of high-drama timing is such fun for your audience that, even if you don't own a Presentation Remote, you still may want to play with it.

Just practice making a clicking motion with your dominant hand as you say the word "click."

Really!

Practice Not Looking at the Screen

It should never, repeat *never*, be necessary to turn your back on your audience.

So always try to have your computer or a "confidence monitor" in front of you on stage when you're presenting. That way, you can verify that you're on the right slide without having to turn your back on the audience to check what's on the screen behind you.

And what (you may be thinking) about when you have to turn around to highlight something with that laser pointer feature in your Presentation Remote?

Don't ever do that either! Instead...

Practice *Describing* What Your Audience Should Look At

Let's face it, if you have to turn around and highlight a portion of your slide with a little red light beam that no one can see, there's way too much stuff on your slide.

But sometimes it just has to be that way, if your firm or your client has pre-set formats.

So when you can't simplify your slide any further and you need to point out one thing among many, try:

- Circling the data point you're talking about in red, so that everyone can see it; and/or
- Telling your audience where to look.

To make this go smoothly, practice what you're going to say; for example, "The number that's circled in red in the third column from the left shows..." or "As you can see in the blue box, upper left corner..."

Giving your audience this kind of direction is much more effective than turning around and waving your hand, or a laser pointer, at the screen.

Practice Putting It All Together

Last but not least, you *do* want to practice delivering your entire speech, with slides, from beginning to end.

By the time you get to this stage, however, it should feel almost like an afterthought (as opposed to being the first and only way that you practice).

If you find yourself thinking, "Ho-hum, yeah, yeah, I know how to deliver all this," that's good!

It means you've practiced *almost* enough.

> Two Things to *Not* Practice

With all this talk about *what* and *how* to practice, there are two things that you should *leave out* of the practicing mix.

Don't Practice Criticizing Yourself

At the start of this chapter, I said that the essence of practicing was to listen to yourself, decide if you like what you're hearing, and keep adjusting until you do.

But don't forget that *evaluating* and *criticizing* are different activities, and that you're doing the former, not the latter.

Evaluating	Criticizing
"I think I may have said that part too fast. Let me try it again, slower."	"You idiot! You're rushing again!!"
"Hmmm. I wonder if that point was completely clear..."	"How's anyone going to understand what you mean if that's the best you can explain it??"
"OK, that was pretty good. Now, do it again."	"Yeah, that'll be *pretty good* when hell freezes over...!"

You get the point. If your thoughts involve name-calling or derisive judgments—if your "self-evaluations" evoke feelings of disdain or hopelessness—you're not **practicing**. What your doing, under the *guise* of "practice," is letting your Nasty Little Voice run wild.

Remember the NLV? It's capable of making thoughtful and intelligent people—people who have valuable things to say—believe that *they'll* never be great public speakers.

And it likes to waylay you as you're practicing. Here are some signs that your NLV is in the house, whether you hear its voice or not:

- Stopping often to correct small "mistakes" (Even if you don't think you're feeling hyper-critical, this behavior is a good indication that you probably are.)

- Feeling disconnected from, or not listening to what you're saying. (Don't practice being disconnected. Remember that you can't connect with your audience if you're not connected to what you're *telling* them.)

- Shortness of breath, palpitations, or other symptoms of low-grade panic. (I'll talk more about Public Speaking Panic in Chapter 11.) While it's good to be able to withstand a little bit of physical and mental discomfort, you don't want to practice feeling panicked while you're speaking.

When your NLV is getting out of control, intruding, or disrupting a practice session, stop!

Take a break. Regroup. Come back later and try again.

> **Step Away from Practicing, Pardner**
>
> I've said, several times, that if you find yourself practicing "wrong," the easiest remedy is to try again later.
>
> You may *want* to keep pushing yourself until you "get it right." But trying to practice when your state of mind is wrong can sometimes make things even worse.
>
> Remember that *being your best self* when you practice is just as important as saying "the right words." So if you've tried but it's just not working, go do something else for a while. Relax your mind and refresh your point of view. Practicing will go better when you come back later.

> Don't Practice Stopping Because of Words!

If you're practicing your speech out loud (and how else would you be practicing it?), you may hear yourself say a word that sounds wrong.

If this happens, *do not stop!*

Stopping at this point will do two very negative things:

- First, you'll be teaching yourself to stop whenever you think you've made a mistake; and second,
- You'll be reinforcing the incorrect view that *word choice is something that really matters.*

Word choice actually couldn't matter less, unless you've chosen a word that is wrong for your technical specialty, or is likely to foment World War III.

(Does it matter to you if I say "kick off" World War III instead of "foment" World War III? Of course it doesn't.)

If you state **the wrong idea** when you're practicing, of course go back and state the right one.

But if you think you've used the so-called **wrong word**, remind yourself that *there is no such thing.* If necessary, tell yourself...

"If my audience is listening, and understands, I must be using the exact right words!"

> If You're Good, You've Practiced. Period.

Often, during one-on-one speaker coaching sessions, I'll rattle off an Instant Speech example, or re-write someone's words on the fly.

Sometimes this really frustrates my clients.

"I want to do that, too!" they'll say. "I want to just open my mouth and speak like you do."

Remember, in Chapter 3, I said to watch out for the word *just*? That caution applies here, too!

"OK," I say. "Let me tell you how I *just* do that."

I then recap how many years I've spent developing public speaking skills, by:

- singing (for vocal control): 12 years of lessons
- playing piano (for rhythm): six years of lessons
- dance classes (coordination): hundreds of classes
- bandleading (stage presence): 18 years of work experience
- writing (general): since I was 6
- writing (speeches): 10 years of 70-hour (or more!) weeks
- bartending (audience management): three years in some pretty rough joints
- pitching: hundreds of pitches
- leading workshops and training sessions: hundreds of them
- speechmaking: dozens of public speeches
- speaker coaching: 10 years full-time, and 10 years part-time before that
- and leading up to, oh yeah, when I'm rattling off an Instant Speech example in a speaker coaching session, *I'm practicing!*

So there ain't no *just* about it.

Now, does this mean you have to do like me if you want to be a great public speaker?

Most definitely not. You'll be a great public speaker when you **Speak Like Yourself... No, Really!**

What it *does* mean, though, is that when you look at someone and find yourself thinking that they're *just* opening their mouths and speaking... don't believe it, 'cause it isn't true!

One way or another, they've put in their time.

› A Final Note: Some Useful Tools for Practicing

The practicing techniques you've just learned (and will revisit in Chapter 9) involve the occasional use of tools.

And since the right tools make any job go easier, I'll close this chapter with a brief list of the tools I find useful, and how you can incorporate them into your own practice routine:

Your Speaking Script

Whether your script is text on paper, a print-out of your slides, or bullets scribbled on the back of a napkin, get it out and plan to read it out loud. (You didn't go to all the trouble of preparing a script so that you could just ignore it, did you?)

Even if your eyesight is good, I suggest printing your script in a 14-to-16 point, clean-looking font with plenty of blank lines and wide margins. (This book is laid out pretty much as I'd lay it out for a speaking script.)

Large, clean fonts and white space will make your script easier to read—and, therefore, easier to practice and deliver.

Your Slides

When you're practicing with slides, you also need to see them clearly.

So put your slide program into full-screen mode. And raise up your laptop or monitor so that, when you're standing, the screen is as close to eye level as you can get it.

(I sit mine on a 12", translucent blue plastic cube.)

A Presentation Remote

I've talked about your "clicker," the little device that allows you to advance your slides without having to touch your computer. I bought mine (Kensington brand) for under $40; it's small, fits comfortably in my hand, and has an operating range of 50 feet.

A Pen and Highlighter

Although it's best to practice without stopping, some of the changes or new ideas you'll think of while you're practicing will be so good you just *have to* stop and write them down.

You'll also notice, as you read through your script, that some important words and phrases could use more emphasis. Use the yellow highlighter to make them stand out so that you emphasize them more on your next read-through.

A Wall Mirror

I like to practice in front of a mirror. I don't use it to excoriate myself—or to bask in how good I look—but to make sure I'm not slumping, shuffling, frowning, or otherwise undercutting my speech with some nervous tic that I could eliminate if I knew about it.

I suggest this, though, with the usual caveat:

If practicing in front of a mirror makes you nervous, tense, or NLV-prone, *don't do it.*

A Timer or Stop-Watch

If your speech must fit into a strict time limit, be sure to time it as you read.

Try using a stop-watch (available at most sporting goods stores for about $10). If you stop speaking, to highlight something or jot down a thought, you can stop the watch and then start it again, which makes timing much more convenient.

A Voice Recorder

You may want to record sections of your speech, or even the whole thing, as you practice.

I've never listened to myself deliver an entire speech straight through; but I do find it useful, if I'm trying to figure out how to deliver a difficult story or section, to record it a few times and listen for what works.

Just don't fall into the trap of thinking that what you sound like on a voice recorder's tiny little speaker is what you'll sound like to an audience.

The same thing is true for videotaping yourself, except even more so. If you want to check on something specific, like how you're moving or what facial expression you're making, videotaping yourself can be useful.

But if you're using video to tear yourself down, or compare yourself to some public speaking superstar... well, you know what I'm going to say!

An Audience of Colleagues or Friends

At some point, late in your practicing arc, you may want to practice with an audience of trusted friends or colleagues.

A "focus group audience"—people you've specifically invited to listen to your speech and give feedback—can help you pinpoint weaknesses, potential problems, issues with your content, and much, much more.

They can also be a wonderful cheering squad, giving you the kudos and encouragement that allow you to stand up before a *random* audience.

But once again, there's a big caveat:

If you're putting together a test audience, don't invite anyone who'll nit-pick you, compete with you, or point out *every little thing* you've left out of your speech that they think you should add.

That kind of feedback, you don't need!

Stage Clothes

It's never a bad idea to practice delivering your speech while wearing the clothes that you plan to wear onstage.

If you're going to discover that your skirt is too short... or your earrings make noise... or your tie distracts people... or your sport coat bunches, you really want to find that out *before* you get in front of people.

In particular, if you plan to wear something unusual—a tux, or maybe six-inch heels—be sure to wear it for at least one run-through.

> Is That It for Practicing?

You would think so, right?

But since you may want to practice other things besides speeches, there's more in Chapter 9.

Take-Away

The activity that bridges *preparation* and *presentation* is called *practicing*. And while many people avoid practicing, the truth is that you can't do your best public speaking without it.

Follow the advice in this chapter to make your practice sessions pain-free and productive—and remember that a few minutes of practicing every day will yield much better results than the occasional all-out push.

Most of all, accept that practicing is a *process*. How (and what) you practice can, and should, change from day to day as you experiment with different approaches, grow your skills, and become more confident.

> Chapter 9

What to Practice When You're Not Practicing a *Speech*

Great public speaking isn't just about making speeches. It includes basic communications skills and the ability to handle other challenges, such as job interviews; media interviews and Q&A; elevator pitches (I'll explain that); introducing yourself at networking or social events; and small talk.

Naturally, there'll be times when you want to practice for these challenges, too—so let's start with your everyday communications skills:

> How to Practice Public Speaking Basics

The kinds of basic communications skills that you can practice daily, without getting near a podium, include:

Become your Avatar	Speak more s-l-o-w-l-y
Pronounce your words clearly	Stand up straight
Pause after each thought	Gesture with your hands
Look your listeners in the eye	Listen to the other person
Smile when you speak	Use shorter sentences
Use Instant Speeches	And pretty much everything else!

And you don't need to face practicing these, or other public speaking skills, alone. Sometimes it's fun to get your friends onboard.

> Your Friends Can Help You Build the Basics

There are two ways to get your friends involved in helping you become a better public speaker: One is to tell them what you're doing, and the other is to keep it a secret.

On the secret side, I often advise clients who are learning to speak more slowly or articulate more clearly to practice on their friends *without telling them.*

It's easy to feel self-conscious when you're changing a long-standing habit like how you pronounce words (which really means: how hard you hit your consonants). So try to slip some slower, more clearly articulated sentences into a regular conversation.

You can make a game of this ("how slow can I get before anybody notices?") And when you discover that your friends don't really notice—or don't think anything of it, if they do—it will put your mind at ease about pushing the experiment even further.

You can also get big benefits from *telling* your friends about what you're doing, and asking them to jump in and help:

- If you want to make more Instant Speeches, teach the format to a friend at work, and see who can use it most in a day.
- If you want to stop saying *uhm* all the time, have your family members poke your arm whenever they hear you saying it.

But the most important reason to tell your friends about your public speaking goals is to gain their active support.

Friends can encourage you to keep at it. They can build your confidence with positive feedback (and they'll often notice the improvements you're making before you do). They can remind you that it's really OK to "just" practice for a few minutes each day, because a few minutes each day will get you where you want to go faster than occasional bouts of intense work.

And your friends and trusted colleagues can serve as your "practice partner" if you need to role play a job interview, or any of the other challenges discussed in this chapter.

> How to Practice for Job Interviews

If you've ever interviewed for a job (and most of us have), you know it's crazy hard to think "on your feet" when you're sweating the intense desire to get hired. Here are some things to think about and practice *before* interview day comes around.

First, the most important thing to understand about job interviews is that they are not *tests*, they are *conversations*. As with any other conversation, your level of success will depend as much on the *connection* you establish with your interviewer as on the quality of information that's exchanged.

> ## Job Interviews: Don't Recite Your Resume!
>
> Because of the types of questions that get asked and answered in a job interview, you might think that you're there to defend or explain your qualifications.
>
> This, however, is just not true. While you should be *ready* to defend or discuss your qualifications, you are not, repeat, **not** at the job interview to prove that you can do the job. (Trust me, they wouldn't be talking to you if they didn't already think you could do it.)
>
> You're at the job interview so that they can decide *whether or not they want to work with you.* So don't obsess about giving "perfect" answers. Remember, your most important goal for a job interview is to connect with your interviewer and have a *conversation*.

Here are the things I recommend you practice for job interviews:

Practice Feeling Relaxed, Confident, Competent, and Friendly

If you don't like to talk about yourself (and if you're an introvert, you probably don't!), you're going to have to put those feelings aside.

You *must* be able to discuss yourself, your experiences, your hopes, dreams, and setbacks in a relaxed, confident, competent, and friendly way.

So add those qualities to your Avatar, and hold onto them (or fake it 'till you make it) as you practice your actual interview content.

Practice Your Stories

The best way to talk about yourself is through **stories**—and what makes a story be a "story" is simply that it has a *beginning*... a *middle*... and an *end*.

In a business context, those translate into:

- **Problem** (Beginning): You identified, or were suddenly confronted with, a challenge, a crisis, or a previously unmet need.
- **Action** (Middle): After appropriate thought, research, consultation, experimentation, etc., you decided on a course of action that you thought would work, and you took it.
- **Result** (End): Thanks to your courage, foresight, wisdom, initiative, etc., the challenge, crisis, or previously unmet need was successfully resolved. (You don't have to *talk about* your courage, foresight, wisdom, initiative, etc., but your story should make those qualities clear.

Here is a story of mine that fits the format:

Problem	Last week, I got a call from a research scientist who was about to be interviewed for a major grant. He was concerned because, although he's an expert in his field, he didn't know how to explain his highly technical work to non-scientists.
Action:	Since time was short, I asked him to come right over. When I saw his cumbersome, 40-slide PowerPoint, I realized that it would take less time to start from scratch again than to edit what he had. So we worked through the Instant Speech format, with me asking lots of questions along the way. Pretty soon, he began to get the hang of using metaphors to educate lay people, for instance, comparing a breakthrough "sticky" molecule to the gluten in bread. At the end of several focused hours, he had a 15-slide PowerPoint that was exciting and easy to follow, and he knew how to practice delivering it.
Result:	Two weeks later, I got a call saying that his project had been fully funded. This was never a slam dunk, because there's a lot of competition in his field. I was very proud that his work, which seemed important and promising (once I understood it!) would continue, with my help.

Stories like this one aren't just illuminating, they're *versatile*. A good one can illustrate many different points, and be used to illustrate many different points. My story shows that I can:

- Create an effective action plan (starting from scratch instead of rewriting);
- Work well under time constraints;
- Translate the technical into the everyday; and
- Produce results for my clients.

Your stories are also versatile. Remember the killer project that you brought in on time and under budget, even though half of your staff had just been laid off? That story could be used to answer these typical interview questions:

- Talk about a time that you succeeded against the odds.
- Do you have experience working with limited resources?
- What kind of a leader are you?, and more

And how about the volatile client that nobody thought you'd ever win over? That story could illustrate persistence, creativity, flexibility, self-confidence, your winning way with difficult people, and many other qualities or skills that prospective employers would value.

Any Story Can Be a Success Story

My clients often find it hard to think of stories that illustrate success. If you have difficulty with this, remember that *success* doesn't have to mean that you won the Nobel Prize or got a lavish year-end bonus. If your client was happy, that is a success. If a problem was resolved, freeing up resources for something else, that is a success. If the actions that you took *didn't work out*, but you learned something important for the future, that part of what happened is a success.

If you emphasize success in the telling of your story, it is, by definition, a success story.

With that in mind, take a minute to list three real-life experiences that illustrate your strengths, skills, or leadership qualities. If you can't think of anything, ask a friend, mentor, trusted colleague, or family member to help prompt your memory.

1 _____

2 _____

3 _____

Pick what seems to be the most promising, or interesting, story of the three, and think about how it fits the three-part structure of *problem*, *action*, and *result*. Ask yourself:

- What is the starting point of this story? Is it when the problem began to develop, when I first learned of it, or when I decided that I needed to act? Why was this problem important? What were the potential consequences?

- What are the actions I took? Did I overcome obstacles to take them? Did I seek advice, organize other people, define the issue, or do other things that showed leadership or initiative? Were the actions that I took simple or complicated, easy or hard? Were they supported by my manager or client, or did I have to prove their value?

- What was the end result of my efforts? Did things change for the better? Was anything learned, by me or others? What might have happened if I hadn't acted? And how did important people react? Was I praised by a supervisor, a client, a colleague? Am I satisfied with the outcome? Would I do things differently if this happened again?

Now that you've explored some of the key points in your story, practice telling it *out loud.*

Keep in mind that your goal is not to give a comprehensive report on every single thing that happened, but to connect with your interviewer and share something that demonstrates why you would be an asset to his or her company.

Practice The Hard Questions

Almost every job interview includes at least one hard question. It's almost as if the interviewer doesn't think he's doing his job right if he doesn't throw you at least one curve ball.

Some questions are hard because they're so generic. Most people hate answering things like:

- Tell us a little about yourself.
- Why do you want to work for this company?

- What's a tough problem that you solved?
- What's your biggest flaw as an employee?
- Why should we hire you?

Other questions are hard because they touch on sore spots (usually, they include the word "why"):

- Why did you leave your last position?
- Why did you drop out of college?
- Why do you think you haven't been promoted beyond the managerial level?
- There are some breaks in your employment history. What were you doing during those periods?

Answers to questions like these—and any others that you find touchy or uncomfortable—should be *prepared in advance.*

Before you begin to prepare them, though,

- Give yourself a quick **attitude adjustment**. Push away any guilt, embarrassment, or awkwardness the question inspires. Remember: Nobody is perfect, and nobody has a perfect job history, let alone a history of constant success. (How well do you think the person who's interviewing you would do if you put *their* bio under a microscope?)
- If you have any doubts about the correct **strategy** to use in answering these questions, consult your A-team of advisor(s) and decide on the best approach. Often, someone else can see an easy solution for a question that has you totally flummoxed.

Now that you know what approach you're going to take, work out and write down your answers to the tough questions. Here are some suggestions that will help with that step:

- Plan to ***answer the question*** before you explain your answer. The more awkward or potentially troubling a particular question is, the more you should prepare to answer it immediately and clearly, *without apology*, but in a way that puts the truth in a positive light. For example...

Question: Have you done much exhibition design?

Answer: I've done some, and I'm looking forward to doing a lot more. Will that be an important part of the job?

[Translation: I've done very little exhibition design]

Question: Why did you relocate to New York?

Answer: I always dreamed of working here, so I asked for a transfer. I had no idea the company was going to close the New York office six months later.

[Translation: Also, I was getting a divorce.]

Question: How are you at taking direction?

Answer: (smile) Pretty good. My goal is always to make a positive contribution to the team.

[Translation: If my manager isn't an idiot, I'll take his or her direction.]

Once your answers are as concise and upbeat as you can make them, keep practicing out loud until you know the answers inside out, and can deliver them while sounding relaxed, confident, competent, and friendly.

And if you need a refresher on *how* to practice, have another look at Chapter 8.

Practice Some Questions You Can Ask *Them*

It's expected that, at some point—often at the end of your interview—the interviewer will ask whether *you* have any questions about *them*.

If the interview has truly covered every question you might have had, it's fine to say, "No, I think you've already answered everything I wanted to ask."

But if that's not the case, it's best for you to ask a few questions to demonstrate your interest in the organization. (If you don't, they're going to wonder what kind of person has no interest in a company she's considering joining.)

The trick here is to *be sure* that your questions couldn't have been answered with 30 seconds of Internet research. "Do you manufacture widgets?" or "How many offices do you have worldwide?" are lousy questions, and will do you more harm than good.

Your best bet is to ask for more information about *something you learned while researching the company;* for example:

- I read that you just opened a state-of-the-art laboratory. What kind of research will be done there?
- On your website, I saw that you stress helping the local community. That's something that I value, and I wondered if all your employees participate.
- Your company has been growing so fast. Do you think that's going to continue? And how does it effect new hires?

Another good approach is to ask for the interviewer's personal take on something that you, as an outsider, could not possibly be expected to know; for example:

- If I'm offered this job, can you describe what a typical day will be like—or is there no such thing as "typical"?
- I'd love to know what you see as the qualities that are most important for succeeding here.
- What's the environment like? How would you describe this as a place to work?

Practice asking these questions just as you would practice answering the ones that you'll be asked—and remember, the point is *conversation!*

> How to Practice for Media Interviews and Q&A

While media interviews and Q&A involve different content then job interviews, they're the same in every other way.

Like job interviews, media interviews and Q&A are conversations in which the ground rules dictate that one person asks a question and the other person answers it. (If both people were asking and answering questions, that would be *small talk*, or plain old conversation).

That's why, in general, you can prepare and practice for media interviews and Q&A in the same way as you would a Job Interview.

In the case of media interviews, however, there is one crucial difference, and that is: **Stick with your Key Message**—and don't be shy about repeating it several times. Remember that journalists are looking for *quotes*.

- If you give them a brief, focused, interesting quote, there's a chance they'll use it;
- If you repeat that quote several times, there's an even better chance they'll use it;
- But if you talk at length about other things, the chances are good that you won't get quoted, or that they'll quote something that's beside the point.

The same thing is true for answering questions during Q&A. Stay focused on your Key Message, so there's no ambiguity about what you think is important.

To prepare for media interviews or Q&A:

- Go back to the previous section and substitute the words "your topic" every time you see the word "you."
- Give particular emphasis to practicing those hard questions. Brainstorm with some friends or trusted colleagues so that you can anticipate, and prepare for, the curve balls that reporters and audience members are likely to throw at you.
- And don't forget to practice feeling relaxed, confident, competent, and friendly. Those traits are just as important when dealing with reporters—or an audience member during Q&A—as they are when you're in a job interview.

> How to Practice Elevator Pitches

If you've never heard the phrase "elevator pitch,"' it refers to the skill of being able to discuss yourself, your business, or your product in the time it takes to ride an elevator with someone.

Why an Elevator?

The idea behind the "elevator pitch" is that someday, you'll get onto an elevator and find that you're alone with *someone who could change your life.* That someone might be your business hero, a rich investor, the CEO of your company, or anyone else that you admire or want to impress; and if this happens, don't you want to know in advance what you're going to say?

Most of the time, of course, you'll be talking about your work to people you meet in other places besides elevators (networking events or social gatherings come to mind). And most of the time, if you're *pitching* your business, yourself, or your ideas, you'll be doing it by appointment, to people you've had a chance to research and think about in advance.

Still, there's just enough truth to the idea that, at any moment, you might need to speak persuasively about your business, that the "elevator pitch" has an important role in people's business imaginations.

And while job interviews, media interviews, and Q&A are all based on answering another person's questions, with an elevator pitches, there is no question. You have to introduce yourself and wade right in.

A Simple Elevator Pitch Format

Let's pretend that this elevator pitch is really happening in an elevator. (In fact, it could happen any place where you know you need to keep things *short*.)

- First, smile, offer your hand, and state your name slowly and clearly ("Hi. I'm Jezra Kaye.")
- Briefly state what you do. ("I'm the President of **Speak Up for Success,** a speechwriting and speaker coaching company.")
- Now state why that's important to them. If you find statements like the following hard to make, practice them in advance so that they roll of your tongue (because you never know when you'll want to say them!):

    "I've trained a lot of successful sales force leaders."
    "I can help your entire company get on message, and speak powerfully about their work."
    "I've helped a lot of top executives build their presence."
    "I give a three-hour workshop that will improve *anyone's* communications skills.

Practice Asking for the Next Step

So far, so good.

But your elevator pitch means little if you don't open the door to following up. If you find it difficult to ask for what you need in business, practice saying things like the following *out loud* and *often:*

> "I'd like to call your admin to set up a brief appointment."
>
> "May I speak with you soon about your company's needs?"
>
> "Do you ever use outside consultants? If so, I'd like to send you my thoughts."

When the Ask is Internal (Within Your Own Company)

If the person you've just met works for the same company as you, focus on getting a brief, private meeting before you reveal any company business.

Even if you think you're alone, *don't* try to explain that you'd love to transfer to their division, or are having trouble with your supervisor, or want to find a mentor, or get on a more exciting project.

Instead, tell them one thing you admire about their leadership or how well their division is performing, and ask if you can make an appointment to speak with them for a few minutes. Making a competent, friendly impression now may lead to an in-depth discussion later; blurting out a complaint or idea probably won't.

> How to Practice Introducing Yourself (for Networking or Social Events)

As an entrepreneur living in New York City, I do a lot of socializing in quasi-business situations. You may also find yourself attending conferences, seminars, networking events, or even parties where people who can be helpful to your career are gathered.

You'd like to meet these people and explore some new possibilities, but you may not be comfortable with *how* to do that.

These situations are similar to elevator pitches, in that—when you meet someone at a networking event or social gathering—you have no way of knowing in advance what's going to interest them, or what the two of you might have in common. (The difference is, you have more time to find out.)

So the last thing you want to do is launch into a speech, even an Instant one. Introductions shouldn't be **speeches**. They're collections of free-standing statements that are designed to test the water and draw interest from the listener.

To illustrate, here's my go-to introduction:

Jezra's Introduction

My name is Jezra Kaye.

I'm a speaker coach.

I show people how to give presentations.

I also write speeches, and help my clients with other communications issues like job interviews, pitches, and small talk.

What you can't see on paper is that the most important part of this introduction is *the pauses.*

I pause after each sentence, to give the other person a chance to ask questions—which gives *me* a chance to gauge his or her interests.

Here are some of the things I commonly hear from people during those pauses:

Jezra's Introduction (with Some Common Reactions)

My name is Jezra Kaye.
- *That's a cool name!*
- *What does that mean?*
- *Where did you get a name like that?*

I'm a speaker coach.
- *You mean, you give speeches?*
- *Are you a speech therapist?*
- *Is that, like, public speaking?*

I show people how to give presentations.
- *So you're a teacher?*
- *What kind of people do you work with?*
- *How long have you been doing that?*
- *Boy, I could really use your help!*

I also work with my clients on other communications challenges.
- *What kinds of other communications?*
- *Do you work on wedding toasts?*
- *Your mean you work for yourself?*

See how every thought can pivot into something else? That's because it's much more important to make a connection than it is to finish your canned remarks!

So when your listener responds to something you've said, *go with it!* Their comment or question isn't an *interruption*, it's the jumping off point for a conversation.

To prepare for that conversation...

Practice Your Attitude

The same attitude that works well for job interviews—being relaxed, confident, competent, and friendly—is perfect for meeting new people, whether in a business or social setting. Your smile, your eye contact, and the interest you show in what the other person is saying are just as important as whatever words you speak, and will pique *their* interest in what you have to offer.

So if you're the kind of person who dreads going out to meet new people, be sure that you practice your attitude as carefully as your words. Take some quiet time to connect with your Avatar, or give yourself a pep talk as you walk into the room. Make sure that the people you meet see someone who's genuinely interested in *them*, not someone who's collecting business cards by rote.

Practice Keeping it Fresh

Over the course of your career, you'll introduce yourself hundreds—perhaps thousands—of times. Through trial and error as well as careful thought, you'll naturally develop stock phrases, stories, and questions that you know are interesting to other people.

But remember that, while you may have said certain phrases over and over again ("I teach people how to give presentations"), the person you're speaking to *has never heard those words before.*

Practice keeping it fresh so that, when the time comes, you can speak with enthusiasm and warmth, even if the words you're saying bore you to death.

This is another example of the role that play-acting plays in successful public speaking. Just *deciding* that you want to feel animated and engaged can often be enough to put you into that frame of mind.

> What to Practice for Small Talk

Roughly half of you who are reading this are scratching your heads right now wondering why *anyone* would need to practice making small talk. You love to talk to new people, and a room filled with interesting strangers looks like a candy store to you.

On the other hand, half of you who are reading this find small talk truly agonizing. That's because small talk neatly combines two activities that both introverts and shy people generally hate:

- Talking about themselves, and
- Talking about things that aren't "important."

Small talk is a variation on the networking introduction I just described, in that you're looking for common ground with a stranger.

The difference is that, while a networking introduction is designed to highlight your professional skills, with small talk, any topic is fair game.

So how do you practice something this open-ended?

By making small talk with another person. Small talk, like interviewing skills, really can't be practiced without a partner.

But, even with a partner at hand, you'll practice more effectively if you understand the object of the game.

Practice Making Small Talk

In spite of the common introvert feeling that small talk exists to torture us, the object of the game is actually quite simple: To keep the conversational ball in play.

Small Talk is Like Tennis, Only the Opposite

Most of us have played games like volleyball, ping pong, tennis, or handball where the object is to hit a ball back and forth until someone misses it and loses that round. In these games, your goal is to hit the ball back to your opponent in a way that makes it *hard* for her to hit it back to you.

Small talk is the opposite. Your goal is to hit the verbal ball back to your opponent in a way that **makes it easy for her to hit it back**, thereby keeping the conversational ball in motion.

What does this look like in action?

1. Hit a verbal volley to the stranger you've decided to talk to. Your opening remark (you can think of it as your *serve*) can be based on something about them, or about the environment or event you're in. If you're at a conference for mystery writers, you could ask, "Have *you* written a mystery?" If you're at a job fair, ask, "Have you been to anything like this before? And did you find it helpful?" If you're on line at the grocery store, you can comment on an item in the other person's cart, or on the length of time you've both been waiting.

2. Once you've spoken, relax and prepare to receive their return hit. Let's say you're waiting to be seated at a new restaurant. You might ask someone who's also waiting whether they've ever been there before (these things are clichés for a reason; they work!). The other person might then reply, "I was here once before. *What about you?*"

Notice that they've given you a nice soft return. The incredibly useful small talk phrase "What about you?" allows you to give almost any answer that occurs to you. This is a phrase you should definitely practice!

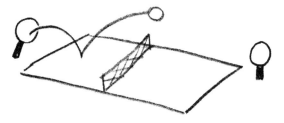

3. You hit their ball back, being careful to *give them something easy to work with*; for example, "I've never been here before. What do you recommend I try?"

4. Your conversational partner (or CP, as Leil Lowndes, author of *Conversation Confidence*,[10] calls them) can reply by giving you a menu suggestion.

---

[10] Author and public speaker Leil Lowndes has written widely on social skills. **Conversation Confidence** is available at http://verbaladvantage.com/programs/start-a-conversation.

At this point, the game is pretty much played out. You can either thank your CP and turn away, or you can start another round of the play by asking them a new question. (They may get to this before you do.)

See how it works?

When you're practicing with a partner, **practice hitting the ball to the other person in a way that will be easy for them to return.**

This means keeping things light, general, and friendly. No conversation stoppers like this one:

> **Person A:** "Do you come here often?"
>
> **Person B:** "No, and I don't think I'm coming back. It's too noisy, and it doesn't look clean."

Similarly, don't get personal in the first few rounds; it's called "small talk" for a reason:

> **Person A:** "Do you come here often?"
>
> **Person B:** "No, but I really needed to get out of the house tonight. I've run out of anti-depressants, and even though I don't have any money, I figured I could probably afford an appetizer."

Okay, then!

Practice Wrapping Up the Game

The other all-purpose small talk skill is tying things up and moving on. To make sure you're comfortable doing that when the time comes, practice phrases such as these:

> "I've enjoyed talking to you, but we should probably go mingle now." (This is one of Leil Lowndes' suggestion)
>
> "It's been nice to meet you. Have a great evening."
>
> "Thanks for the conversation! I hope you enjoy your dinner."

Practice Smiling

Just as with most other forms of communication, the underlying secret for making successful Small Talk is to show the other person that you like them and appreciate spending a few minutes in their company.

To that end, don't ever practice without a warm smile on your face—one that reaches to your eyes!

And don't forget: The point of small talk is not to be smart, suave, or unforgettable.

The point is to keep the conversational ball moving, and to show the other person that you enjoy playing this game with them, and are glad the two of you have connected.

And Now, Back to Your Speech

Congratulations! You've learned how to prepare a speech that's valuable to your audience, and practice it powerfully.

You've also seen that the fine art of practicing can apply to improving your basic skills, or to challenges like job interviews.

Now it's time to go back to your speech, and tackle the final **Speak Like Yourself** step: Connect with Your Audience, and Present with Pride.

Take-Away

To be the best public speaker that you can be, practice your basic communications skills, in addition to preparing for presentations. Your friends can help you (knowingly or not!) work on basic skills like speaking more slowly or articulating more clearly.

You'll also want to practice for communications challenges like job interviews; media interviews & Q&A; elevator pitches; networking introductions; and small talk. Because it's so hard to think "on your feet" in these situations, prepare your comments, questions, and answers, and practice them out loud in advance.

But also be aware that your *attitude*—relaxed, confident, competent, and friendly—is critically important; sometimes more important that what you're actually saying.

Chapter 10

Connect with Your Audience and Present with Pride

My Nightmare

The night before I finished the final edit of this chapter, I dreamed that I was supposed to be singing at a gala event, in a major hall.

I used to be a jazz singer, so that part of the dream wasn't scary for me. The scary part was that, when I arrived at the hall on the night of this performance, I had no idea *what* I was going to be singing, *with whom*, *when* in the program, *where* I was supposed to go to check in, or anything else that I would normally expect to know at either a singing or a public speaking gig.

To make things worse, the show was in progress, no one was on hand to give me information, and I was literally stumbling around in the dark looking for help. (And that's before the part where I found out that I was scheduled to perform in a *dance* routine!)

My nightmare wasn't a fun experience; but fortunately, it's an easy one to avoid.

In this chapter, you'll find out how to prepare—logistically, physically, and mentally—for the day when you present your speech (henceforth known as Speech Day).

By the time you stand in front of an audience, you'll be ready to focus on what *really* matters: Connecting with them, and presenting your speech with the confidence and pride that it deserves.

› Logistical Prep for Giving a Speech: Who, What, Where, When

Up until now, this book has focused on the first two Speak Like Yourself steps:

Speak Like Yourself Step 1: Prepare a Speech that's Valuable to Your Audience

Speak Like Yourself Step 2: Practice Delivering It Powerfully

Both of these can be accomplished more or less in isolation. You can understand your audience without leaving your office. And you can practice in the privacy of your own home.

But now the entire game's about to change. That's because **Step 3: Connect with Your Listeners and Present with Pride** requires that you *go somewhere*—even if "somewhere" is a conference room down the hall from your office—and interact with *someone*.

To pull this off, you'll need to know, at minimum:

- **Where** am I speaking, **how** will I get there, and **how long** will that take?;
- What **time of day** is my speech, and what is happening **before and after** I speak? (This matters because an audience's energy, like an individual's, is very different at 11AM than it is at 4PM; and it's very different if people have been sitting for two hours than it is if they've just had a break);
- **When** am I expected at the venue (place where you'll be speaking), **who** will meet me, and **what** will happen between then and when I give my speech? (Find out in particular if you'll be able to get onstage for a "**tech rehearsal**" with microphone and slides; but also find out things like: Will you be expected to sit through other speeches? Meet with VIPs? Join your hosts for dinner? etc.); and most importantly,
- **Who** is my point person? Know who you can turn to for help or information *in advance* of Speech Day, and *on* Speech Day, at the venue (they may not be the same person.

The Most Important Thing of All: Your Point Person's Contact Info

This chapter includes lots of lists of things that you "should" know, do, and take with you before you give a speech. But only one of these is truly indispensable, and that is: Be sure that you know how to instantly and reliably reach your point person. (A word to the wise: Get their phone number. An email address isn't good enough.

Who is that? Your Point Person is the person who knows what's going on at the speech site. The person who can answer all your questions. The person who will help you with any difficulties that arise before, during, or after your speech.

With their help, you will come out right even if you misremember your speaking time, bring the wrong notes, or end up in a parking lot in New Jersey instead of at the venue (I've done all these things). Without it? All I can say is: Best of luck!

If you already nailed down this information *when you first agreed to give the speech,* all you need to do is be sure you have it on hand now. But if Speech Day is approaching and you still don't know the answers to the questions above, *don't panic.*

It's never too late to pick up the phone. Do it now; I promise you'll feel better.

> Physical Prep for Giving a Speech: Your Checklist

It's not enough for *you* to arrive at the venue on Speech Day. You also need to be sure that you, and whatever tools you may need, arrive there in good shape and ready to work. So...

Pack What You Need the Night Before

I've learned the hard way that it's better to get up everything ready the night before you give a speech than to wake up the next morning and have to frantically scramble for what you need.

I also suggest that you create a list of the items you may want to take with you, and check them off as you gather them.

Here's my list:

- **Logistical information**: My point person's contact info; directions to the venue; the names print-outs of any other instructions; an agenda for the event;

- My **speaking notes**, with the pages numbered, in a labelled folder;

- My **computer**, or a stick with my speech on it, or both (*bring this even if you've sent your speech in advance; it's amazing what people can lose!*);

- **Connector cords**, in case I end up having to connect my Mac to their projector;

- My **presentation remote** ("clicker"), in case I don't like theirs;

- **Pens**, **paper**, and a **yellow highlighter**, in case I want to take notes on what the speaker who presents before me says, or mark something in my speech to emphasize. (Note the difference between *editing*—which is futile at this point, and squanders energy; and *adapting in response to what's going on in the room*);

- A printed copy of how what I'd like delivered for my **Introduction**, in case the person who's introducing me has lost the copy I sent by email;

- **Hand-outs**, if I'm producing them instead of the event organizers (or even if they are, as back-up);

- **Sign-up sheets**, if I'm planning to collect email addresses;

- Hand-written **thank you cards** for the event organizers and/or my clients;

- A big stack of **business cards** to give to event participants;

- A **sweater** (conferences are often over-AC'd);

- Flat **shoes** (because who wants to wear heels during tech rehearsals?);

- A bottle of **water** (not everyone offers this);

- **Cough drops**, **kleenex**, a **toothbrush** if it's a long day, my asthma **meds**;

- A protein **snack** so I don't hit the stage hungry;

- **Casual clothes** to wear on the way home;

- **Chocolate**, to enjoy on the way home; and,

- A romance **novel**, for the moments before my speech that I'll spend hiding in the Ladies' Room pretending this is all a dream. (If you're an Extrovert, you probably won't need this one!)

Choose What You're Going to Wear in Advance

In Chapter 8, I suggested that you practice in the outfit you'll wear onstage. Not only is this a great practicing tip, it's a good way to make sure you pick your stage clothes early. This is especially useful if, like me, you're prone to waking up late and just throwing "something" on.

Choose your clothes carefully—because all your hard work and preparation can be seriously undermined if you end up wearing things that just don't work. With that in mind:

- Watch out for tight waistlines, restricted shoulders, crazy patterns, jewelry that clinks, skirts that are too short (if you're standing on a stage, you're going to be *above* the audience), and pants that ride up to reveal dorky socks (unless you're speaking to techies, in which case, go for it!). Bright, solid colors work well, as long as they're not gaudy.
- If you're a woman, I'm going to strongly suggest that you *never* wear all black clothes when you speak. While all-black (the New York businesswoman's standard uniform) makes you look serious in a meeting, it makes you fade away visually onstage. Red, deep blue, or another eye-catching color is a much better choice.

And women, one other consideration:

Sometimes, as a public speaker, you will be given what's called a Lavallier ("lav") microphone instead of a hand-held mike or one that's attached to a podium or on a table stand.

"Lavs" have two parts that each must be secured to your clothing:

- The microphone itself gets clipped to the collar of your shirt, suit or dress; so choose a collar or neckline with enough substance to hold it in place (no gauzy, floppy tops). In addition,
- The lav runs on a battery pack that must also be clipped to your clothing. The usual choice is to clip it to your belt or waistband, or to the back of your collar if you're wearing a dress. And if none of that works, you can either hold it while you speak, or clip it to your pantyhose or underwear (assuming that you're wearing either). These are not happy solutions.

But lest you think this is all about gadgets, here's some advice that your mother might have given you:

On Speech Day, Eat a Good Breakfast

I mean a *good* breakfast. Public speaking is incredibly hard work, and starting the day with your version of brain food—whether that's eggs and grits, or soy milk and granola—will help get your day off "on the good foot."

It's no accident that many of the items in my list of things to pack, above, are emergency food rations. Remember that your 2:00 PM speech could easily get rescheduled to 4:00 PM (You skipped lunch? Isn't that a shame!).

And drink lots of water early in the day, so you can stop drinking a few hours before your speech. That way, you won't have to run to the bathroom, but you also won't be dehydrated.

› Mental Prep for Giving a Speech: Get Ready to Connect With Your Audience

The most important preparation for Speech Day is getting yourself in the right frame of mind. After all,

- You're worked hard to get to this point.
- You've mastered lots of new skills.
- And now you're going to stand in front of an audience, and present your thinking to them.

That's the goal: Connect with your audience, and present with pride.

But no matter how hard you've worked, how well you've prepared, and how much you've practiced, this final step can feel like a daunting challenge. That's why it's good to remember (and spend some time thinking about) one simple fact:

You *Know* How to Connect with People

Unless you've lived your life in a cave, there are dozens—perhaps even hundreds—of people in the world who feel connected to you. They range from your best friends and family members to casual but familiar acquaintances like the check-out girl at your grocery store or the guy who makes UPS deliveries.

Think about what connects you to each of these people:

- Some connections are based on shared *experience*. This may describe the people you grew up with, or people who've lived through the same life events as you.
- Some are based on shared *beliefs*, including the religious, political, and social ideas you cherish.
- You probably have friends who share your *interests*. If you coach a Little League team, or love taking cruise ship vacations, or spend your weekends doing Civil War Re-enactments, chances are good that you have friends who share those passions.
- You may be connected to several *communities*. Your child's school, your place of worship, the neighborhood you live in, and your job are common community connections.
- And you may connect with others through your *identity*. Identity can include myriad factors such as race, class, the region where you grew up, your education, sexual orientation, and much more.

Now think about the *audience* you're going to speak to.

Do you share an interest, a profession, an ideal, an experience, a community, a point of view?

Any and all of these connections—no matter how strong or ephemeral they may be—can open your audience's hearts and minds and pave the way for a *public speaking relationship.*

That relationship will continue to grow as you treat both your audience and yourself with respect. Your best attitude is the one made famous by the title of Thomas A. Harris's self-help book ***I'm OK—You're OK***.[11]

Because the best public speaking relationships grow in the soil of mutual respect.

[11] ***I'm OK—You're OK***, by Thomas A. Harris, MD, HarperCollins Publishing, 1967, 2004.

Respect is the Magic Ingredient

There are several stories in this book about speakers who thought they were better or smarter than their audiences—the animal researcher in Chapter 1 and Department of Education representation in Chapter 3 come to mind—and those stories didn't end well.

Similarly, if you think your audience is better or smarter than you, that won't end well, either. (And by the way, if they're so much better or smarter than you, why did they invite you to speak to them?)

The Gifts that You Bring to an Audience

Up until now, we've talked about *your content* as the primary gift that you bring to an audience.

But don't forget that, in addition to the value your content provides, you also bring very personal gifts that have developed throughout your entire life—and that give your audience myriad different ways to connect with you:

- **Mind**—Some of your listeners will respect your thinking;
- **Body**—Some will enjoy the way you speak, or how you move when you're onstage;
- **Mission**—Others will admire the passion, or the sense of purpose that drives your speech;
- **Style**—Still others will respond to your personality, your sense of humor, or the personal stories you tell.

And, of course, many listeners will appreciate, admire, or be intrigued by how you function in *more than one* of these overlapping areas!

In Chapter 1, you listed three or four strengths or skills that became the basis of your Avatar. Those were your *public speaking gifts*.

Gifts that I Bring to an Audience

Mind: _____

Body: _____

Mission: _____

Style: _____

While it's not always possible to channel your thoughts, particularly in the face of public speaking fear, it's worth on _connection_ and _gifts_ instead of on Speech Day anxieties!

And while you're doing that mental preparation...

Bring On Your Avatar

Like a guardian angel, pinch hitter, or superhero, your Avatar has been patiently waiting in the wings for his or her "close-up" (the moment when he or she could shine).

Now that moment has come, and—ideally—you can sit back and relax, knowing that your Avatar has this whole public speaking thing covered:

- After all, he isn't thrown by a little bit of queasiness.
- She won't succumb to low-grade panic.
- He won't let anything shake his confidence.
- And she won't forget that her job is to connect with the audience and present with pride.

As a complicated human being, you might be tempted to... well, complicate the public speaking experience. But your Avatar knows that everything is under control. After all,

- You've prepared a speech that's valuable to your audience.
- You've practiced delivering it powerfully.
- And now, all you have to do is trust yourself, get up onstage, and give it your best.

❯ Speech Day: What To Do When You Hit the Stage

Let's start with what *not* to do.

Even if every cell in your body is screaming at you to hurl yourself at the podium and start talking the second you get there, don't!

Doing this will put you off-balance, like a sprinter who starts off on the wrong foot. Sure you can recover, but it's better (as the old adage has it) to begin as you mean to go on. So, instead:

- Walk onstage in a relaxed and confident way;
- Put your notes down on the podium;
- Stand solidly, with your feet apart and your knees slightly bent;
- Look at the audience—yes, *really* look at them! See? They look pretty friendly, don't they?;
- Take a slow breath and let it out;
- Remind yourself that your Avatar is present, and has everything covered;
- Wait until you feel calm, confident, and powerful.

Now you're ready to begin speaking!

The Power of Picking Your Moment

You've probably seen athletes resist tremendous pressure—from the time clock, the fans, the announcers, and sometimes their own team members—and *stand there until they're really ready* to throw that pitch, or jump that hurdle, or lift that weight, or serve that ball.

Good public speakers do the same. Pick your moment and begin powerfully.

› Eye Contact—The Difference Between Speakers and Talking Heads

You may have been told that the best way to deal with fear of public speaking is to *look over the heads* of the people you're speaking to.

While there's something bizarrely tempting about that advice, please ignore it and do the reverse: Look your listeners in the eye, connect with them, and accept the positive feedback they're giving you.

That's right; positive!

Most people avoid looking their listeners in the eye because they're afraid of what they're going to see. They're afraid they'll discover that the audience is bored, or restless, or filled with contempt.

But the likelihood that you'll see any of those things is very, very low indeed. Because, with very few and rare exceptions, the people who are listening to you *want you to succeed.*

Some of that is generosity; but most of it is enlightened self-interest. They want to listen to a *good speaker*, and if you're the person they're listening to, they want that good speaker to be you.

That's why, given the slightest opportunity, most audiences will show that they're on your side. They'll pay attention. They'll nod or smile. They might even make a note or two.

But you won't notice any of that unless you're *looking at the audience!*

Eye contact has two main functions:

- One is to remind your listeners that *you're talking to them*, and
- The other is to remind *you* that your audience is listening!

So do everyone a favor and close the feedback loop by looking into your audience's eyes.

Of course, this raises an interesting question...

How Do You Make Eye Contact with Lots of People?

The truth is, you only have to make it with one person at a time. (Which is good, because you only *can* make real eye contact—the true-blue, looking them right in the eyes kind of contact—with one person at a time.)

It's strange but true that, if you're looking straight into *one person's eyes,* everyone else in your audience will feel as though the eyes you're looking into are theirs.

This paradox goes along with the larger truth that *there's no such thing as a big audience.*

From your point of view as a presenter, it looks like you're talking to a lot of people. Most of us, when we speak to a group, are acutely aware of whether that group comprises 10, 100, or 1000 individuals. And most of us experience greater anxiety as the number of warm bodies mount.

But *from your audience's perspective*, each person in the room experiences your presentation as if it's being delivered to him or her alone. That's because each person:

- Hears you separately;
- Reacts to you individually; and
- Is actively responding to the points you make in the privacy of his or her own thoughts.

What you'll see, when you meet one person's eyes, *is that they are just one person.* They're hearing your words, and reacting to your thoughts, as an individual—not a mythic, 40-headed beast.

Finish the idea that you're expressing, and now look at another person.

See? Same thing!

No matter the number of bodies in front of you, you are really only speaking to *one person.*

So focus on your audience of one, and try to relax.

> **What if Someone *Doesn't* Look Positive?**
>
> If you look at someone who *doesn't* look positive, just move your eyes to someone else. There's no need to torture yourself by trying to connect with negative people when most of your audience is delighted with your speech.

And get ready to settle in for a nice chat.

> You've Planned Your Work, Now Work Your Plan

Lots of people love variety.

But when you deliver your speech, there is a big difference between a little creative improvisation and impulsively throwing away your plan.

One is good (let's call it variety); the other is not (let's call it a train wreck).

If you get up in front of an audience planning to say, "It's a pleasure to be with you in Cleveland today," and you decide instead to say, "You know, this is my first trip to Cleveland, and I have to say that it's the friendliest, cleanest, and most well-organized American city I've ever been to," that's *improvising*. You're making a change, *within the context of your larger plan*, that's based on something that changed in real time (you got to know Cleveland).

If you get up, however, and say, "I was going to speak with you today about how we can improve our domestic sales, but I've decided to focus on our sales in the Middle East instead," that is *not improvising*, it's throwing your speech out the window—and perhaps your reputation with it.

While you may want to adjust your opening, or ad lib an occasional comment, or skip a particular story, or elaborate more on a particular point, **please do not change anything basic**.

And by "basic," I mean **your Key Message** and **the structure of your speech**.

- Changing your Key Message is an invitation to disaster, because whatever message you *think* seems more inspired in the heat of the moment is unlikely to actually be better than the one you've spent the last few weeks perfecting.

- And changing the structure of your speech is a good way to strand yourself upstream in a canoe without a paddle. You're suddenly inspired to discuss your third Supporting Point before delivering your Key Message? That's great—except your audience won't understand it fully, because you haven't laid the groundwork yet. And, oh by the way, when you reach the place where you *would have* discussed your third Supporting Point... what are you going to talk about?

You've put a lot of effort into creating a success plan for this speech. So when you finally get up on stage, in front of people, work the plan that you've carefully created.

Instead of juggling ideas or making changes to your program, concentrate on connecting with the audience, and delivering your speech with pride!

Take-Away

Like the other two Speak Like Yourself steps, Step 3: Connect with Your Audience, and Present with Pride is not a matter of chance. The more carefully you prepare yourself—logistically, physically, and mentally—the more you'll be able to stay in the moment and receive the positive feedback you've earned. Remember that your speech is a gift to the audience, as are your special qualities of mind, body, mission, and style. So stay in the present, work your program, and get ready for your speech to succeed!

> Chapter 11

Public Speaking Panic

In a sense, this entire book has been about how to combat fear of public speaking, through preparation, practice, and having a game plan that will work.

Still, because this is real life, you can do your audience analysis; prepare an absolutely superb speech; practice within an inch of your life; prepare yourself logistically, physically, and mentally to connect with your audience and present with pride; and *still* experience public speaking panic when the time comes to take the stage.

It's not fair. It's not right. But it's possible, because—while it's not true that most people would rather be dead than give a speech—public speaking does kick up some serious qualms in the vast majority of people.

Whether it manifests as ongoing anxiety or panic attacks, managing this fear can take a big chunk or your time, energy, and attention.

> What Public Speaking Panic Feels Like

Public speaking panic—it used to be called *stage fright*—can be a powerful and unsettling experience, particularly when it strikes unexpectedly.

You can't breathe. Or you can't think. Your heart pounds, or you lose feeling in your fingers. The physical sensations can be bad, and the feeling that you're losing your grip, that you're about to crash and burn in public, is much worse.

This is panic—and it can strike even the best-prepared public speakers.

No matter how conscientious, experienced or well-practiced you are—and no matter how eager you are to speak to a particular audience—*anyone* can have a bout of stage fright.

Why does this happen?

We don't know, any more than we know what *déjà vu* really is, or how a winning athlete can suddenly hit a slump.

We know that fear comes from the amygdala—part of the pre-verbal, limbic section of our brains that's sometimes called our reptilian mind— and that it's part of the fight-flight-or-freeze response that was designed to make us run from hostile warriors and hold still when a lion was near. But what, exactly, triggers this unscheduled mental experience?

Emotion and memory are clearly involved. Stress appears to be involved... or maybe it was something you ate for breakfast. You can't know for sure, and it doesn't really matter.

What *does* matter, if you do suffer from either an ongoing or a momentary bout of public speaking panic, is that **it doesn't mean anything.**

That's really important, so let me repeat it:

Fear of public speaking doesn't mean anything.

- It doesn't mean that you're going to fail.
- It doesn't mean that you're an imposter.
- It doesn't mean that you're underprepared, or that your speech sucks, or that you're kidding yourself.

The only thing that public speaking panic means is that *you're human, and you're feeling fear.*

> Get That NLV Out of Your Head

While it's useful to be able to tolerate a *little* fear of public speaking (after all, you sometimes have to tolerate a headache or other distraction while you work), it's not useful to let your Nasty Little Voice run wild.

Left to its own devices, the NLV will fill your head with thoughts that *seem* rational, but are actually just stealth attacks of the sort we discussed in Chapter 8. These might include:

"I'm not ready."

"My speech sucks."

"I can't believe I thought I could do this!"

"Who would want to listen to *me*?"

Even while you're giving your speech—and getting a *great* reaction from your audience!—the NLV may still keep at it, trying to undermine your self-confidence with pronouncements like:

"No one's smiling; they must really hate this."

"That was a pretty stupid point I just made."

"Oh, God, I just said *uhm*!"

"Why isn't this over yet?"

In the famous words of First Lady Nancy Reagan, *just say no* to thoughts like these.

Taking your fear seriously—*believing* what it tells you—is like being the teenager in a horror film who opens the door to a psycho ax murderer.

And strangely enough, this is not an extravagant comparison. Your NLV is like nothing so much as it's like a psycho ax murderer: cruel, bloodthirsty, and completely irrational.

So keep that mental door *shut*!

> To Panic Is Human, to Make Mistakes Is, Too!

With apologies to Alexander Pope, who wrote, "To err is human, to forgive, divine," it's also human to *worry* about erring, a/k/a making a mistake.

Isn't that what stage fright is? The worry (felt more in our bodies than our minds) that we might (a) make an error, and (b) suffer for it?

So let's dispense with the "I might make a mistake" thing right away.

There's no might about it; you **will** make a mistake. (Remember the part about being human?) Maybe you'll:

- Forget a word, a phrase, a point, a story;
- Talk too fast, or shuffle too much, or stand in a less than flattering way;
- Respond ungraciously to a question, or take a drink of water and spill some on your shirt.

There are endless possible ways to not meet your audience's expectations—or your host's, or, worse, your own—and *you're not going to get through a speech without making at least one of them!*

Fortunately, mistakes don't count, because *nobody cares* that you're not perfect. (If you were perfect, you'd almost certainly be safe, boring, and irrelevant.)

What counts is that you *keep going*, as you did when you were practicing, and *stay focused on giving your best.*

> ## Yeah, Yeah... But What Do I *Do* if I Panic??

What you do if you panic is *reconnect with yourself.*

Not the self of your birth certificate or bio, but the self behind your Avatar. The self that we discussed in Chapter 10, that brings multiple gifts to your audience. The self that...

- Can handle life's challenges;
- Has prepared conscientiously to give this speech well; and
- Is temporarily obscured by panic, but can be reclaimed.

To get in touch with the full power of that self, call on each of the parts of yourself that we discussed in Chapter 10:

Mind

Think about other times in your life when you felt fear, but did the thing you were afraid of anyway. (Arguably, that's the definition of courage.)

Everyone has had these successes. Can you remember one of yours? Do you recall how you pushed through the fear? Would that technique be helpful now?

Often, we already *know* how to manage our fears—but when fear strikes, we forget that we know this. So ask a trusted friend to remind you. Put a sign up at your desk, or write a memo ("BREATHE") on your speaking script.

Your mind can also help by replacing NLV "thoughts" with thoughts that are true:

- Remind yourself that you've worked hard on this speech, and are positioned to succeed;
- Remember that *you* are the person your audience wants to hear from. *You* are the person who can best convey what you know and believe in. *You*, in other words, are the right person for this job; and last but definitely not least,
- Think about how happy you'll be when your speech is over and has been a success. (I like to picture a glass of white wine, but be sure you don't *drink* the wine until you're through speaking!)

Another useful approach is to actually examine the assumptions behind your fear. In their excellent workbook, **Mind Over Mood**, cognitive therapists Dennis Greenberger and Christine A. Padesky[12] explore how errant thoughts can trigger our emotions.

Consider what happens when you think each of these things:

> **Thought A:** "I made a mistake. I'm a total failure. What's the
>   use of even trying?"
>
> **Thought B:** "I made a mistake. I learned something that will
>   improve my performance next time."

In the first case, your mood will drop, your energy will drop, your self-esteem will drop... it's downward spiral time. But the second thought might actually *raise* your energy, your mood and your self-esteem, because you've put your experience into a positive and powerful context.

Two similar thoughts that relate to public speaking might be:

> **Thought A:** "I'm nervous about this speech. That proves I
>   totally suck, have no idea what I'm talking about,
>   and am going to bomb."
>
> **Thought B:** "I'm nervous about this speech. That proves I care
>   about my topic, respect my audience, and want
>   to do well." (Or: "That proves I'm a conscientious
>   employee." Or: "That proves I value competence."
>   Or: "That proves I want to have fun.")

The first thought gets you halfway to a panic attack.

The second thought will help get you to the stage.

And like so many things about public speaking, the beauty of taking a *mind over mood* approach is that you can practice the skill anytime, anyplace.

When a negative thought pops into your mind, practice taking a different point of view. Instead of, "I screwed that up, so I'm obviously no good at it," practice thinking, "Oops. I didn't do *that* perfectly!"

And practice smiling while you think it.

[12] **Mind Over Mood: Change How You Feel by Changing the Way You Think**, by Dennis Greenberger and Christine Padesky, The Guilford Press,1995

Body

Again, call on whatever experiences you've had of calming and centering your body to help you cope with the physical symptoms of fear. Here are some things that I've found useful:

- If your fear shows up as a physical symptom, practice describing it neutrally. ("Oh, wow. I'm loosing sensation in my arms. I guess I'm nervous about this speech!") Practice smiling while you think it.

- Label the intensity of the symptom (and your fear in general), on a scale of 1-5, where 1 means you feel like throwing up, and 5 means you feel like disintegrating, like the crew of *Start Trek* does when they get "beamed up."

- Familiar or repetitive movements—stretching, yoga, or deep breathing—can have an almost hypnotic effect that may help dispel the physical stress.

- If you're a physically active person, build some hard exercise into your Speech Day, or do some jumping jacks or jogs in place while you're waiting to take the stage. (Another good reason to wear comfortable clothes!) Just be sure you leave yourself enough reserves to get through the energy-burning main activity of the day, giving your speech!

- I also find that *shaking off the fear* helps me dispel physical tension. (Picture how a dog moves to shake water off its fur, and you'll get the idea.) This looks silly, but it's very effective; try it in private and see what you think.

In other words, make this stuff a game: Set up a point system. Give rewards for Fear of the Month. Nervous Tick of the Week. Crazy Thought of the Day. Favorite Physical Symptom.

Be silly. Be creative. Let fear know you're not afraid of it.

Mission

Hopefully, when you agreed to give this speech, your mission, or sense of purpose, was engaged. Knowing that you're speaking for a reason that's larger than yourself can be tremendously energizing (look at the power of gospel music!), and can minimize your personal fears.

Of course, the reality is that, on your job, you may be speaking because you were "volunteered." But even if that's the situation, it's greatly to your advantage to *find something* about this speech, this content, or this audience, that activates your sense of purpose. (Appendix C has more on how people with different public speaking personalities think about their missions.)

Your audience may well relate to, or even be inspired by the sense of purpose that you convey. But more importantly, *you* may find that you have more strength and courage to speak on behalf of a larger goal than you otherwise might have.

And if this speech just doesn't inspire a sense of mission, let *the public speaking relationship itself* give you purpose.

Make it your mission to connect with your audience... to connect *them* with your content... and to give the best of yourself all around.

Style

In Chapter 10, we talked about how your personal style makes you uniquely interesting to an audience.

It also makes you uniquely able to fight off public speaking panic. So take a tip from your style of social interaction, and:

- If you're shy, or an introvert—someone who prefers small, intimate gatherings to big, noisy ones—find a private place where you can read, reflect, or give yourself a pep talk before getting on stage. Being alone can often help introverts or shy persons connect with their sense of mission, and fortify themselves against fear.

- If you're outgoing, or an extrovert—someone who enjoys stimulation and likes to be in the social whirl—you can psyche yourself up in the opposite way: By meeting the people who'll be in your audience, interacting with them, and making friends before you get up to speak to them.

Style is also one of the things you've built into your Avatar. You've given him or her the personal qualities you want to emphasize in yourself; so calling on your Avatar is probably the best and fastest way to re-connect with the strengths of your personal style.

Whatever you do, don't let fear of public speaking trick you into leaving *yourself* at the stage door.

Because your audience wants you to *Speak Like Yourself*.

No, Really!

Take-Away

No matter how well you've prepared and practiced, it's possible to feel panic before giving a presentation, because panic comes from a pre-verbal part of your brain that has no relationship to reality. Use every tool in your toolkit—from deep-breathing to self-talk to jumping up and down or physically shaking off the fear—to put this meaningless reaction in its place. Trust the hard work you've done so far, and don't be seduced by your Nasty Little Voice. Instead, rely on your preparation, your Avatar, and the special gifts you bring to your audience to help you *Speak Like Yourself*.

> **Chapter 12**

You *Can* Speak Like Yourself—and Succeed!

By now, I hope you've discovered that *you* can be a great public speaker.

You've always had the *potential* to **Speak Like Yourself**—to deploy your strengths and skills; your mind, body, mission, and style.

And now, you have the ability and tools to do it right.

So here, for quick reference, are the take-aways from each chapter in this book. Use them as reminders and guides as you keep moving down your own public speaking path.

> Chapter 1: To Be or Not To Be...*Me!*

While many people feel that they *should* speak differently, that perception comes from a nasty little self-critical voice (NLV), and not from the realities of what it takes to be a good public speaker.

In reality, speaking like *your best self* is the fastest route to success; and it starts with appreciating your existing communications strengths, skills and qualities. These will become the basis for your public speaking Avatar—a streamlined version of *the best of yourself* that can help you in every public speaking situation.

Defining and naming your Avatar is the first step toward becoming the kind of public speaker that *you* want to be.

> Chapter 2: "Doomed to Fail" vs. "Speak Like Yourself"

The way that most public speakers go wrong is by leaving *people* out of their equation. A speech that is built around a title or topic can never be as rich or persuasive as one that's built with a particular audience and their needs and interests in mind.

That's why you should avoid the Doomed to Fail approach that begins with a data dump, involves not practicing, and ends with putting your head in the sand.

Instead, in the rest of this book, you'll learn how to execute each of the three **Speak Like Yourself** steps: (1) prepared a speech that has value for your audience; (2) practice delivering it powerfully; and (3) connect with your listeners and present your speech with pride.

> Chapter 3: Understanding Your Audience

Public speaking success is based on your audience's perception that you've delivered value *on their terms*. To do this, you must know who you're talking to, and what they want.

You also need to know what *you* want from them. Armed with this knowledge, you can look for areas in which your audience's needs and your own needs overlap.

Even in difficult situations, you can succeed if you've thought about your audience. Ask yourself: "Who are they (in relation to my speech)?" "What do I want them to do, or do differently?" and "Why should they care (what's in it for them)?"

> Chapter 4: Your Key Message, a/k/a The Big Key

Your Key Message (a/k/a The Big Key) is the core points of any communication, large or small. It should be big, true, important, have personality, and relate your interests to those of your audience members.

Test your message by asking, "If this is *the only thing* my audience remembers, have I made my point?" and "If my audience believes that this Key Message is true, am I closer to getting what I want?"

If the answers to both questions are *yes*, you're well on your way to creating a speech.

› Chapter 5: Turn Your Key Message Into an Instant Speech

It's easy to turn your Key Message into an Instant Speech that will serve you in situations like job interviews, as well as presentations. To do this, add two, three, or four Supporting Points ("buckets") to your Key Message.

These Supporting Points should meet audience expectations by going together, building on each other, or being random.

And don't forget to "bracket" them by repeating your Key Message at the end of your Instant Speech. Doing so will create a balanced and authoritative presentation that sounds professional, and will ensure that your most important point is the last thing your audience hears.

› Chapter 6: Grow Your Instant Speech into a Full-Length Presentation

It isn't hard to grow an Instant Speech into a full-length presentation. Most of the expanded length will come from new material added to your Supporting Points (and if your Supporting Points become long or complicated, turn them into mini-Instant Speeches, for better comprehension). But you'll also need to add an Attention Grabber, Preview, Recap, and Close to create a fully rounded experience for your audience.

Take a flexible approach to how much of your speech you'll write out versus delivering from bullet points. Only script out the places where you'll need to use exact wording; and be aware that what you need to be prompted on may change as you practice your speech.

Finally, don't forget that, while an Instant Speech is your best starting point in most public speaking situations, there are exceptions to that rule.

› Chapter 7: Don't Be Afraid of PowerPoint

While lots of people love to hate PowerPoint, it can be a flexible and useful tool at many stages of the speechmaking process: It's a good outlining tool; it can give you an overview of your speech; and, as you'll see in the next chapter, it can help you learn your speech.

The key is to use each slide to support just *one* of your ideas in a way that helps hold your audience's interest. Don't put your speaking notes in your slides, because doing so means that you've given up your role as the *presenter*. And if your slides depict data, be sure they do it in a way that illuminates rather than obfuscating your point.

If you keep those tips in mind, and put some thought into creating it, PowerPoint and Keynote can *enhance* your public speaking instead of detracting from it.

> Chapter 8: Practice Makes Perfect... But Only If You Practice Right

The activity that bridges *preparation* and *presentation* is called *practicing*. And while many people avoid practicing, the truth is that you can't do your best public speaking without it.

Follow the advice in this chapter to make your practice sessions pain-free and productive—and remember that a few minutes of practicing every day will yield much better results than the occasional all-out push.

Most of all, accept that practicing is a *process*. How (and what) you practice can, and should, change from day to day as you experiment with different approaches, grow your skills, and become more confident.

> Chapter 9: What to Practice When You're Not Practicing a Speech

To be the best public speaker that you can be, practice your basic communications skills, in addition to preparing for presentations. Your friends can help you (knowingly or not!) work on basic skills like speaking more slowly or articulating more clearly.

You'll also want to practice for communications challenges like job interviews; media interviews & Q&A; elevator pitches; networking introductions; and small talk. Because it's so hard to think "on your feet" in these situations, prepare your comments, questions, and answers, and practice them out loud in advance.

But also be aware that your *attitude*—relaxed, confident, competent, and friendly—is as important as what you're actually saying.

› Chapter 10: Connect with Your Audience and Present with Pride

Like the other two **Speak Like Yourself** steps, **Step 3** is not a matter of chance. The more carefully you prepare yourself to **Connect with Your Audience**, and **Present with Pride**, the more you'll be able to stay in the moment and receive the positive feedback you've earned.

Remember that your speech is a *gift* to the audience. Whether they connect with you through your special qualities of mind, body, mission, or style, they are as eager to see you succeed as you are to bring value to them.

› Chapter 11: Public Speaking Panic

No matter how well you've prepared and practiced, it's possible to feel panic before giving a presentation, because panic comes from a pre-verbal part of your brain that has no relationship to reality.

Use every tool in your toolkit—from exercise to self-talk to deep breathing—to put this meaningless reaction in its place. Your preparation, your Avatar, your relationship with the audience, and your commitment to speaking like yourself will help you withstand fear, and deliver a great speech!

› Chapter 12: You Can Speak Like Yourself— and Succeed!

What's the recap of *this* chapter?

It's simply that you've now learned everything you need to know in order to **speak like yourself**, and succeed.

What's more, if you keep working at this, I'm willing to bet that you'll wake up one morning and discover that you *like* public speaking!

And why wouldn't you?

You're leading with the best of who you are, and delivering well-considered content to an audience that appreciates it—and you.

That's the gift of **speaking like yourself**.

> **Appendix A**

Instant Speech Worksheet

As you use more Instant Speeches, at work and in your daily life, the format will become second nature. (And don't forget, it's easy to grow an Instant Speech into a full-length presentation!)

This worksheet takes you step-by-step through the process.

First, focus on your audience

Before you can prepare a speech that's valuable to them, you have to know who they are! So ask and answer the following questions.

A. WHO am I speaking to?

_____

_____

B. WHAT do I want them to do (or do differently)?

_____

_____

C. WHY should (will) they care about what I'm telling them?

_____

_____

Find Your Key Message

Now that you've analyzed your audience, ask, "What's the biggest, most important thing I want them to know about my topic?" (To refresh your memory on Key Messages, see Chapter 4.)

_____

_____

Supporting Points

Support your Key Message with two to four points or discussions. These Supporting Points are like buckets that you can fill with as much or as little information as you'd like, depending on the length of your presentation. Choose those topic areas now, and list them on the lines below.

1. _____

2. _____

3. _____

When you create a speech, filling these buckets will demand more time and attention. But for now, let's finish laying out the *structure* of your presentation, so that—whether it becomes an Instant Speech or a full-length presentation—you'll have a complete template to follow.

Close

One of the "Key to the Key" tests described in Chapter 4 is, "If my audience believes this Key Message, will I be closer to getting what I want?" You've created first a Key Message, and now a speech that has moved the audience toward what you want; so **ask them for it** in your close.

_____

_____

_____

Attention Grabber

Now that you know what's in your speech, what will you do at the very beginning to pique your audience's interest? Write down your idea, and practice it out loud to see *how it works in action.*

_____

_____

_____

_____

> INSTANT SPEECH WORKSHEET

START BY THINKING ABOUT YOUR AUDIENCE, not about "what you know." Ask:

A. WHO am I speaking to?

B. WHAT do I want them to do (or do differently)?

C. WHY should (will) they care about what I'm telling them?

**NOW WRITE YOUR PRESENTATION, starting with #1, and working through to #5.
(To *deliver* it, start with the Attention Grabber, and continue straight through to the end.)**

5. ATTENTION GRABBER (a question, strong statement or surprising fact related to your topic)

1. KEY MESSAGE (the most important thing you're telling your audience)

2. SUPPORTING POINTS (1-3 buckets of facts, stories, questions, etc. that support the message)

2a.

2b.

2c.

3. KEY MESSAGE (use basically the same words as #1; the difference is, now you've proven your point)

4. CLOSE (be very specific about what your audience should do next)

> Appendix B

The Resources I Use Most

There are many classic public speaking resources, but this list skips them to concentrate on the books I've bought six times because I'm always giving them to clients, the videos I constantly recommend, and the ideas I couldn't do without. All of them are easy to find online.

> Public Speaking

- On my site, ***www.SpeakUpForSuccess.com***, you'll find hundreds of blog posts on the topics in this book, as well as answers to Frequently Asked Questions and information about speaker coaching.

- The public speaking book I recommend most often (and my favorite, besides the one you're reading) is ***Make Your Point! Speak Clearly and Concisely Any Place, Any Time***, by Bob Elliott and Kevin Carroll, Bloomington, Indiana: Author House, 2005.

- Thanks to **YouTube** and the **TED** series ("Ideas Worth Sharing"), there are now unlimited numbers of presentations posted online. Many TED Talks will inspire you and give you models to copy. Two that I recommend are by **Susan Cain** and **Brené Brown**. Search for their names and "TED" on YouTube; they're the ones with five million plus views.

- ***A Woman's Guide to the Language of Success***, by Phyllis Mindell, Ed.D., Prentice Hall Trade, 1995 reveals how some women and men undermine themselves with weak words and communications habits—and how to stop.

- ***How to Get Your Point Across in 30 Seconds or Less***, by Milo O. Frank, Pocket Books, 1986. The name says it all; a treasure.

- ***Conversation Confidence***, an audio course by Leil Lowndes, available at www.verbaladvantage.com. Ignore the 1980s style, and focus on her excellent tips.

> Personality Theory

- **Please Understand Me**, by David Keirsey and Marilyn Bates, Prometheus Nemesis Book Company, Del Mar, CA, 1984. (**Please Understand Me II** is by Keirsey alone).

- To learn about the Myers-Briggs Type Indicator®, I recommend the very readable **Type Talk: The 16 Personality Types that Determine How We Live, Love, and Work**, by Otto Kroeger and Janet M. Theusen, Dell Publishing, New York, 1988.

- **Mind Over Mood: Change How You Feel by Changing the Way You Think**, by Dennis Greenberger and Christine Padesky, The Guildford Press, 1995. This workbook will help you root out negative thoughts that can create public speaking fear.

> For Job Seekers

- **What Color is Your Parachute**, by Richard N. Bolles, Ten Speed Press (updated yearly; old ones are fine). Check out the advice about resumes, positioning your accomplishments, and informational interviews. There are also accompanying workbooks, including one for teens.

> For Everyone

- **The Art of Procrastination**, by John Perry, Workman Publishing Company, Inc., New York, 2012. This book is short, funny, and revelatory. It will change how you think about preparing a speech, even if you don't procrastinate.

> Appendix C

Reliable, Helper, Improver, or Experiencer: Discover Your Public Speaking Personality

Since long before I studied social psychology at the University of California, Berkeley, I've been interested in personality.

And while **Speaking Like Yourself** is mostly about being your best as an *individual*, it also has a *group* dimension. That's because public speaking challenges aren't all personal. We share some of them with the millions of people who, like us, are primarily Reliables, Helpers, Improvers, or Experiencers.

So if, like me, you're fascinated by the way that personality influences our feelings, thoughts, and actions, you'll find this introduction to public speaking and personality theory— based on insights from the **Myers-Briggs Type Indicator®** and the **Keirsey Temperament Theory™**—a useful supplement to the rest of this book.

> From Black Bile to MBTI: The Four Human Personalities

The idea that there are four basic types of human personality has been around for thousands of years.

It shows up in astrology (astrological signs fall into four groups: earth, air, fire, and water), and in early medical philosophy (Hippocrates, the father of modern medicine, thought that our temperaments came from four bodily fluids: black bile, yellow bile, blood, and phlegm).

It also shows up in my public speaker coaching.

The modern version of this theory first appeared when psychologist David Keirsey published the temperament theory he'd been developing since 1940.

Just after Keirsey's book was published[1], the Association for Psychological Type was founded. APT's mission was to promote, and continue studying psychological type, including the **Myers-Briggs Type Indicator® (MBTI®) assessment**—a personality instrument that Isabel Myers, with her mother Katharine Briggs developed over a *fifty year period* beginning in 1923.

The MBTI® assessment, based on the personality theories of psychologist Carl Jung, sorts people into 16 personality types, based on how they prefer to re-charge their energy, gather data, and make decisions.

And, in one of those confluences that benefits everyone, David Keirsey's four temperaments mapped neatly onto the 16 Myers-Briggs personality types, making it possible for people to think *specifically* about their MBTI® type, and more generally, about their Keirsey temperament.

That temperament is the basis of your Public Speaking Personality.

❯ Which of these Four is Most Like You?

Keirsey called his four temperaments Guardians, Idealists, Rationals, and Artisans. In this book, I call them **Reliables**, **Helpers**, **Improvers**, and **Experiencers**.

What's in a Name? What You'd Like to Be

It's hard to sum up a diverse, multi-faceted group of people in one word, but I wanted to try for names that were easy to "get" without knowing much about temperament theory. After much thought, I've chosen names that indicate what each group *values*, in themselves and others.

It's not that Helpers are more helpful than other people, that Reliables or more reliable, that Improvers make more improvements or that Experiencers experience more (or more deeply). It's that ***these are core values each group aspires to***, and standards against which they judge themselves.

---

[1] ***Please Understand Me***, by Keirsey, David and Marilyn Bates, Prometheus Nemesis Book Company, Del Mar, CA, 1984.

Keirsey illustrated the four temperaments using the characters from a beloved story, **The Wizard of Oz**.

In this timeless and archetypal tale, four friends go on a quest through dangerous territory. Though they're deeply bonded, their goals are quite different: Dorothy wants to get home; the Tin Woodsman wants to get a heart (gain compassion); the Scarecrow wants to get a brain (become wise); and the Cowardly Lion wants courage to do great deeds.

These four different goals tell us a lot about what each temperament yearns for:

- As a **Reliable**, Dorothy values home, family, community, hard work, responsibility, and tradition. Her desire is to return to Kansas and the institutions that anchor her life.
- The Tin Woodsman, a **Helper**, wants to *feel* more passionately. He dreams of living his values, making a difference, and helping other people.
- An **Improver**, the Scarecrow cares about gaining competence through education. His goal is to think wise thoughts and solve complex problems.
- And the Cowardly Lion, who's an **Experiencer**, wants to be a man (or rather, lion) who lives life fully, in the moment, without holding back.

Of course, nobody falls *exclusively* into any one of these categories; we're all much too complex for that.

But Keirsey's Temperament Theory and the Myers-Briggs Type Indicator do a great job of describing the mix of priorities and preferences that underlie our personalities, and that inform our choices throughout our lives.

So whether you're predominantly a Reliable, Helper, Improver, or Experiencer, your *public speaking personality* gives you an invaluable way to think about your own communication preferences and priorities (which often translate into strengths and weaknesses). It also provides a guide for how to best communicate—and *not* communicate—with people who have different personalities.

As you read the four sections that follow, think about the people you communicate with regularly. When those communications are strained, some of these insights may provide help.

My Husband and the Milk

My husband, a Reliable, is very literal-minded. He's also attuned to his physical environment. So if I've left milk out on the kitchen counter, he's likely to ask me, "Is there a reason why you left the milk out?"

For years, this question made me furious. Even though he said he was just asking for information, it sounded to me like he was criticizing my housekeeping. (Did I mention that Helpers tend to take things personally?)

After studying the MBTI, I realized that my husband really was just asking for information. So, the next time he asked, "Is there a reason why you left the milk out?" I said, "Yes. It's out because I forgot to put it away."

He nodded, put the milk away, and that was that.

> Reliables: Taking Care of Business (and Everything Else)

Are You a Reliable?

Reliables are the people who "make the trains run on time." Buttoned-down and respectful of tradition, they can often be found in large, hierarchical workplaces like corporations, national non-profits, or the military. And the closer you get to the top of the ladder, the more Reliables you'll find, because their ability to make decisions and give (or follow) orders makes them invaluable to the organization.

If you prefer to work at a solid organization that offers security and a clear chain of command, you may well be a Reliable; close to four out of 10 people, equally male and female, are.

More than any other personality group, Reliables are concerned with doing what "should" be done. Their commitment to traditional values is their greatest strength, making them loyal, responsible, and determined to protect the institutions they value. They deeply believe that the world would be a better place if everyone just did what they were supposed to do.

The downside to that attitude can be an impatience with other people's inattention to rules, schedules or procedures. Reliables truly don't understand why others lack the discipline, focus, or persistence to just do what's "right." Former First Lady Nancy Reagan, who famously counseled people to *Just Say No* to drugs was probably a Reliable.

If You Have the Reliable Public Speaking Personality

One of the toughest lessons for a Reliable communicator to learn is that your calm logic and reasoned proofs may not be sufficient to persuade people with different Public Speaking Personalities.

To reach the widest audience, begin to build some of these elements into your presentations and other workplace communications:

- **Likability.** Helpers want to like you, and if they like you, they are more inclined to find both you and your ideas credible. So approach them in a friendly manner. Smile, engage them, and ask them questions. Be interpersonal when you can; and, above all else, let the Helpers that you communicate with know that you notice and value their contributions.

- **Competencies.** Your credentials mean little to an audience of Improvers. This group will test you with questions, doubts, and skeptical push-back—even if they agree with you! If you demonstrate competence (in their terms), if you persist in being thoughtful and accurate, if you value practical new ideas, it's likely that you'll pass the test—until the bar gets raised tomorrow.

- **Engagement.** More than the other three groups, Experiencers value living in the moment. To reach them, don't just stand there, *do* something. Sensory elements, experiential training, movement, and concrete experience are your path to an Experiencer's respect.

Tips for Talking to a Reliable

If you're not a Reliable, but must persuade one, remember their preferences, and try to speak:

- **Calmly.** Reliables are not swayed by your passion for a suggestion or idea. They want to see your research. Facts, figures and calmly spoken logic are the best ways to make your case.
- **Responsibly.** Remember that, for Reliables, serving and protecting the important institutions in their lives is key. If you can't point out a true benefit to the institution, you probably won't win them over to your idea.
- **Historically.** Because Reliables have a high level of comfort with doing things the way they've been done before, consider citing precedents for whatever you're proposing.

A Classic Clash: Reliables and Helpers

Following Hurricane Katrina, one of my clients—the Executive Director of a non-profit foundation—was frustrated with her Board Chair. She had developed a great new program for delivering services in the Gulf region; but for some reason, her Board Chair was hesitant to sign off on the plan. In fact, the more passionately my client argued that they had to bring expanded services to people in the Gulf region, the more hesitant her Board Chair became, even though he shared this goal.

The key to unraveling their conflict turned out to be temperaments. My client was a Helper, and her Board Chair seemed to be a Reliable. When she switched her approach and showed him how her plan could be implemented *without creating financial stress for the foundation*, he was happy to approve the increased expenditure for a cause they both valued.

> "Why Can't We All Just Get Along?!"

Are You a Helper?

Helpers are a smaller group than Reliables (about 12% of the population, versus 38%), yet they make a big impact through their passion for improving the world by helping others. Committed to living by their values—whatever those values may be—Helpers are emotionally intense people who despise conflict and tend to take things personally. They deeply believe that the world would be a better place if everyone was just kind and compassionate.

Because 70% of Helpers are women, and because they often work in cooperative or "soft-skills" areas such as teaching, HR, or fundraising, Helpers aren't always taken seriously by people for whom competition is king. But superstars like Oprah Winfrey, women's clothing designer Eileen Fisher, and (it's thought) Presidents like Ronald Reagan have clearly shown that values-driven Helpers can be just as successful in business and the public sphere as anyone else.

If you rely on emotional intelligence; if you think a lot about how you treat others; and if you're drawn to work that fulfills your values, you may be a Helper.

The great communication strength of Helpers is their uncanny ability to intuit and respond to the feelings and needs of others. This strength can become a weakness, however, when Helpers get trapped inside their *own* emotions, or decide that they're going to "save" another person who may not even want their help.

If You Have the Helper Public Speaking Personality

One of the toughest lessons for a Helper to learn is that values-based arguments will not seem persuasive to many people who aren't Helpers. So to reach the widest audience, begin to build some of these elements into your presentations and other workplace communications:

- **Objectivity:** In addition to learning to sound objective, cultivate the skill of viewing your audience objectively, and guard against a tendency to over-react to perceived conflict. If, for example, your audience isn't responding to a particular idea, don't jump to the conclusion that they hate it (or, worse, hate you!). The more you can separate *yourself* from *your ideas*, the more effective you'll be as a speaker, because you won't take disagreement as a personal judgment.

- **Practicalities:** Other Helpers may favor an idea because it's right; but everyone else wants to know it's also *workable*. (And "everyone else" is 88% of everyone.) Be prepared to explain the practical implications of your ideas, and to present a clear and reasoned argument for why they should be adopted.

- **Boundaries:** The desire to like and get along with people can sometimes blind a Helper to real differences. So hold your empathy back a bit, and listen before jumping in. Ironically, you'll communicate better when you're more objective about other people.

Tips for Talking to a Helper

If you're not a Helper, but must persuade one, remember their preferences, and try to speak:

- **Personally.** Helpers view "objectivity" as coldness and disconnection; the harder you try to persuade them with logic, the more you'll persuade them that you have no personal stake in your ideas. So be sure to speak about the topic at hand from your personal, as well as your professional, point of view.
- **Cordially.** The key to winning a Helper audience is to get them to *like you*—and that's much easier if you genuinely *like them*. What makes a Helper audience willing to listen and, ultimately, believe is the personal tie they feel to a speaker; so do your best to set a tone of mutual appreciation and warmth.
- **Helpfully.** Helping others is a Helper creed. Don't talk to them about how your idea will save money or revolutionize your field until you've first explained how it will make the world a better place for the people and values your Helper audience holds dear.

> Making the World Safe for Continuous Improvement

Are You an Improver?

Like Helpers, Improvers are a small group, just 12% of the U.S. population. But their impact is out of proportion to their numbers, because Improvers like to invent, innovate, and improve the systems that run our lives (think Steve Jobs). Seventy percent of Improvers are men; but male or female, they share a respect for intuition and creativity with their Helper "cousins."

What Improvers want most is to be more Improver. They also want *you* to be more Improver, and will push hard to make sure that you are. An Improver boss can be quite a challenge, because—no matter how well you performed yesterday—today is a new day, and the bar has gone up.

If you admire continuous improvement, and are drawn to fields that reward a mix of objectivity and innovation such as IT, entrepreneurship, or the law, you might be an Improver.

The big communications strength of Improvers is their ability to "read" complex patterns, and to develop creative solutions to problems that others may not have even noticed. But that strength can seem like a weakness when others can't keep up with the Improvers thinking. In that case, an intellectually-demanding Improver may come across as impatient, dismissive, or cold.

If You Have the Improver Public Speaking Personality

By now you've probably noticed that the biggest communication challenge for each of the four public speaking styles is understanding (or perhaps *putting up with*) the ways in which the other three Personalities talk and think.

So to reach the widest audience, begin to build some of these elements into your presentations and other workplace communications:

- **Simplicity:** Learn to take an argument apart and walk people through it, step by step. Although it's more fun to jump into the middle, you'll leave your audience in the dust before your presentation has even begun.

- **Personality:** Your audience wants to know and like you. Just stating the facts is not enough, particularly if your listeners interpret your objectivity as arrogance or detachment. Make a few comments about yourself. Mention your passion for this topic. It won't undermine your credibility; it will make you seem less intimidating.

- **Humility:** Nobody wants to be reminded that you're probably the smartest person in the room. So when you're pointing out why your ideas are *right*—leave out the part about how everyone else is *wrong!*

Tips for Talking to an Improver

If you're not an Improver, but must persuade one, remember their preferences, and try to speak:

- **Rationally.** Although Improvers are independent thinkers, they respect objective decision-making. The best of both worlds, for them, is a creative idea that's supported by a solid analysis or strategy.

- **Competently.** Too many speakers want their credentials or experience alone to serve as a statement of competence, but with Improvers, it doesn't work that way. They'll only listen if you make sense, so do your thinking carefully, and be prepared to justify your position.

- **Fearlessly.** Expect to be tested by an Improver audience, and accept the challenge with gusto. They will respect you for it.

- **Systemically.** Like Helpers, Improvers are concerned with creating a better future. But where Helpers focus their efforts on people, Improvers focus theirs on *systems*, objective ideas, and logic. Everything from computer architecture to fixing the country's infrastructure are fair game. If you want to capture a Improver's interest, talk to them about transforming a system.

> "I'd Rather Be *Doing* Something"

Are You an Experiencer?

Like their "cousins," the Reliables, Experiencers are a large (38%) group, made up equally of men and women. But unlike Reliables, who are often rewarded with power, wealth, and leadership positions, Experiencers are often underestimated.

That's because the Experiencer is action-oriented, and cares more for doing something that feels real in the moment than for pushing papers or sitting at a desk. They may be the smart kids who get bad grades because they won't sit still; and as adults, they're drawn to fields like fire fighting, sales, or pre-school teaching, where problems are concrete and pay-offs are immediate.

If you believe that life should be fun; if you pride yourself on living in the real world; or if your job is more actual than abstract, you may be an Experiencer.

An Experiencer's greatest communications strength is his or her ability to assess what needs to be done *now*, and convey it with clarity and confidence. That strength can become a weakness, though, if an Experiencer neglects the big picture and lets spontaneity veer into recklessness.

If You Have the Experiencer Public Speaking Personality

For Experiencers—who are practical and action-oriented—speaking up may seem like a waste of time. But actions don't always speak louder than words, and if you neglect to add your voice, an important perspective will be lost.

So to reach the widest audience, begin to build some of these elements into your presentations and other workplace communications:

- **Efficiency:** If you're the person who's running a meeting, try making everyone stand throughout it. Milo O. Frank[2], who pioneered this technique, swore that it cut *every* meeting down to half an hour or less. (And if you're not the person who's running things, make them a present of Frank's book.)

- **Follow-Through:** You may get more satisfaction from leaving your options open than from making decisions that close off possibilities. Still, business depends on finishing things, so develop your tolerance for making decisions and following through.

- **Diplomacy.** If you find yourself chafing when Reliables talk about rules and regulations, or Helpers talk about values and ideals, or Improvers talk about systems and logic, try to stretch your patience a bit. *Then* tell people, in a diplomatic way, that perhaps the team would benefit from a little more action and a little less talk.

[2] *How to Run a Successful Meeting in Half the Time*, Frank, Milo O., Simon & Schuster (June 1989)

Tips for Talking to an Experiencer

If you're not an Experiencer, but must persuade one, remember their preferences, and try to speak:

- **Practically.** You've seen by now that each public speaking style has its own preferred way of gathering information. Helpers want to hear the big picture. Improvers want to hear about the structure. Reliables want to hear the facts. Experiencers want the facts, too, but only the ones that have practical application. An exhaustive review of every fact that's known on a topic will drive them crazy.

- **Flexibly.** Just *talk*. Canned communication is suspect to this group. One of the things Experiencers excel at is flexibly changing course when reality demands it. That's why they're the people you want to follow if your building catches fire during a meeting; it's also why someone who rigidly sticks to his script without incorporating what's going on in the moment is not going to win the hearts and minds of Experiencers.

- **Concretely.** Say what you mean, say only what's necessary, and then let people get out of there.

Your Public Speaking Personality Meets Your Mission

In Chapter 11, I mentioned that one of the ways to combat public speaking panic is to activate your sense of mission.

Mission can mean quite different things to the four Public Speaking Personalities, and the chart that follows gives examples. But whatever mission means to you, there's much to be gained and nothing to be lost from the sense that you're speaking for a larger purpose.

Public Speaking Style	Ideas to Activate Your Sense of Mission
Reliables may be motivated by a sense of duty and care for the institutions they belong to	"I have a duty to give the best speech I can. I've organized my ideas effectively, and followed best practices in preparing and practicing this speech. I have the right credentials to speak to this audience, and the information I'm presenting will benefit them and their organizations. I will not let undisciplined feelings prevent me from doing my best."
Helpers may be motivated by a desire to help other people lead more fulfilling lives	"It's possible that someone in my audience will experience a pivotal or transformative moment because of something I present. I'm not going to let my fear get in the way of sharing the important and potentially life-changing information that I've worked so hard to prepare for this audience. I'm going out there and touch their hearts!"
Improvers may be motivated by a desire to improve systems, and increase the competence of themselves and others	"Let's face it, not too many people have the insights and original perspective that I'm about to offer this audience. It would be silly to let some irrational fear get in the way of sharing the information I've put together for them. It's possible that this speech will help people improve their performance; it's certainly going to help me improve mine!"
Experiencers may be motivated by a love of experience, of living life fully in the moment	"I came here to have some fun, and that's what I'm going to do, fear or no fear!"

Another Dimension of Personality: Introverts and Extroverts

You've probably heard of "introverts" and "extroverts"—but you may be surprised to learn that these words have nothing to do with being *outgoing or shy*. Introverts can be outgoing and extroverts can be shy because these categories aren't about sociability. They're about how people *recharge their energy*:

- **Introverts** recharge their energy *internally*, so they are very attuned to their inner world of thoughts and feelings, ideas and beliefs. They can enjoy a big party (for a while!), but generally prefer to socialize in smaller groups, or with intimate friends. They may feel overloaded by physical stimuli (light, sound, movement, even temperature) that have no impact on their extrovert peers.
- **Extroverts** recharge *externally*, in the outer world of people, places, and things. They can enjoy quiet time (for a while!), but generally prefer to socialize in larger groups ("the more the merrier" is an extrovert expression, as is the comment by 20th century humorist Will Rogers that he never met a man he didn't like.)

How to Spot an Outgoing Introvert

I once mentioned, at a workshop I was leading, that I'm an introvert—and nobody believed me. One participant asked, "Is there a behavior we could observe that proves it?"

"Sure," I said. "We just took a break, right? How many of you talked to someone?"

Almost everyone's hand went up.

"And how many of you talked to *me*?"

This time, no one's hand went up. No one had talked to me during break because, while most of them were recharging with small talk, I was reading in an empty office, recharging in my introvert way.

There's also a big difference in how introverts and extroverts communicate:

- **Introverts** hold their ideas close. They prefer to speak only when they have something important to say; and even then, they may hold back if an idea isn't fully formed in their own minds. They prefer silence to small talk, and don't understand how extroverts can go on and on discussing seemingly unimportant things.
- **Extroverts** love talking for its own sake, and may not know what they think about something until they hear themselves saying it out loud. They prefer sound to silence, and don't understand how introverts can choose quiet over communicating.

As Susan Cain has pointed out in her influential book **Quiet**[3], the playing field for these two groups is not level. Study after study has shown that Extroverts are judged more positively than Introverts on a range of competencies and leadership skills. Because they talk more, it's assumed that they know more.

So what's an Introvert to do? Here are some tips:

Make Yourself Speak Up in Meetings

Before you go into a meeting or any other situation in which ideas will be presented and discussed, *decide* how many times you're going to speak up. (I suggest three: once near the beginning of the meeting, once near the end, and once at a place of your choice in the middle.)

Do this because, if you don't speak up, many of your colleagues or clients will assume that you have nothing to contribute. So jot down a thought that occurs to you and look for an opportunity to state it. And remember that no one but you cares if the thought is *stellar*; it only has to be *good* to succeed.

Play Strong Within Your Limits

At conferences or networking events, limit your participation time rather than your enthusiasm. I used to dread these events because I thought I had to stay for the entire time, forcing myself to glad-hand, work the room, and collect what felt like dozens of business cards (usually, it was just five or six).

How did I convert that chore into a pleasant challenge? By giving myself permission to pop in for 40 minutes and then leave. Now I can enjoy my networking time, knowing that I'll probably meet one interesting person.

Come Out as an Introvert

Since Susan Cain's book, it's become much easier to announce that you're an introvert, and I recommend doing this. For one thing, it educates your colleagues. For another, it helps manage their expectations. I now routinely say things like, "This has been fun, but I'm going home to be an introvert," or "You know, my introvert side doesn't do well at parties, but I'll try to drop by for a few minutes."

Quiet: The Power of Introverts in a World that Can't Stop Talking, by Susan Cain, Crown Publishers, New York, 2012.

Letting people know in advance that you appreciate their company but plan to set limits lowers the pressure on you to conform, and the likelihood that others will be offended when you take your marbles and go home.

So, Introverts, you now have strategies.

But what about extroverts? How can you be more inclusive—and why should you?

Here's why: Making the world more welcoming for Introverts isn't an act of charity on your part. It's a way to bring the talents of 45% of your colleagues more fully into focus, so that you can benefit from their contributions.

Here are some strategies that will help:

Extroverts, Make Yourself Speak *Less* at Meetings

The same strategy introverts use to speak up will help you to speak a little *less* at meetings, informal discussions, and brainstorming sessions: Three times during each meeting that you attend, refrain from saying something you would otherwise have said.

The space you leave might allow an introvert to enter the fray. And if you're the person *running* the meeting, hold back the extroverted participants and invite someone who hasn't spoken yet to contribute. You may need to push a little, but if you hold to the expectation that *everyone* should contribute, your team's Introverts will begin to open up.

Meet Your Introvert Colleagues Half Way

Business, networking, even social events are often organized for the convenience of Extroverts. If you want to be part of a fully functioning team, though, it makes sense to consider *everyone's* comfort:

- If you're speaking to a colleague who wants to sit in a quiet corner instead of standing in the middle of a crowded room, go with her.
- If a team member prefers small group discussions to town hall-style meetings, consider accommodating his idea.

- If a colleague wants to leave a gathering when you think the party's just begun, accept and understand—and be ready to explain to others—that this doesn't reflect on his or her team spirit. It reflects on the state of their energy, which is drained by participating in extrovert events.

Learning to Make Room for Introverts

I recently moderated a panel with five participants. Four of them were extroverts, and one was a pseudo-extrovert—Susan Cain's word for Introverts who are good at "passing."

Early in the panel, the pseudo-extrovert spoke up. But as time went on and the true extroverts began to joust more seriously for the limelight, she got more and more quiet. As the moderator, I should have been drawing her out; but, even knowing better, I found myself assuming that she was quiet because she had nothing to add. It was shockingly easy to make this mistake.

Later, she corrected me, saying, "I *did* have comments to make, but everyone else was talking so much that I thought *somebody* should hold back."

It is almost always the Introvert who thinks that "somebody (i.e., them) should hold back. If we accept that choice at face value, we're losing their experience and unique perspective—and everyone is poorer for it.

Afterword

I'm not usually a fan of the "journey" concept, but with public speaking, it really *is* all about putting one foot in front of the other. You move a little bit today... a little bit tomorrow... and pretty soon you're standing in a different place than you were when you started down the path.

Many of my clients gawk at me when I tell them that public speaking will be fun. "Have fun," I say, about their presentations. "Yeah, sure," they reply. (*Like that's gonna happen.*)

But here's the thing: It *will* happen.

If you keep working, this will gradually become fun, because it's fun to be dynamically engaged. It's fun to have a kick-ass skill. It's fun to know that what you say is important to your audience.

So go out there and have some fun!

And best wishes for the journey.

CPSIA information can be obtained at www.ICGtesting.com
Printed in the USA
BVOW09s1842200715

409597BV00002B/4/P